THIS, THAT,

BUT MOSTLY

THE OTHER

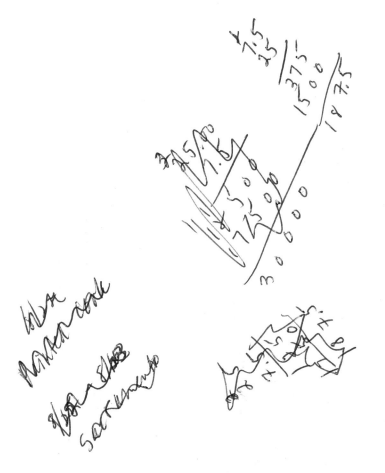

THIS, THAT, BUT MOSTLY THE OTHER

LISA WARING

TATE PUBLISHING
AND **ENTERPRISES**, LLC

Published by Tate Publishing & Enterprises, LLC
127 E. Trade Center Terrace | Mustang, Oklahoma 73064 USA
1.888.361.9473 | www.tatepublishing.com

Tate Publishing is committed to excellence in the publishing industry. The company reflects the philosophy established by the founders, based on Psalm 68:11,
"The Lord gave the word and great was the company of those who published it."

Book design copyright © 2015 by Tate Publishing, LLC. All rights reserved.
Cover design by Rtor Maghuyop
Interior design by Jomel Pepito

Published in the United States of America

ISBN: 978-1-63449-122-8
Biography & Autobiography / Personal Memoirs
14.11.24

To my best friend and loving husband Mike who has always believed in me, encouraged me, shared my dreams, and remained my greatest champion.

Contents

Introduction

Life is a great teacher. Our journey through life brings with it experiences that yield pointed lessons. What we learn from those lessons, great and small, help us gain our personal perspective and better understand our purpose and place in the world.

Unfortunately, our lives are busy. Getting through our daily routines becomes a priority, leaving little time to reflect on the important experiences in our life and how they have shaped who we are and what we have become.

I am not a famous historical figure, a movie star, a well-known politician, or person of great monetary wealth. Like most people, I am just an ordinary person who leads an ordinary life. Through deep reflection, I have come to learn that my ordinary life has been filled with extraordinary blessings.

Several years ago, I was asked by the editor of our small hometown newspaper, the *Sandspur*, to write a weekly column. I was given full discretion to write on any topic that I wished. Every week, I would sit down and write a story I thought would be of interest to others.

While writing, I often found myself drifting away into memories of my childhood and family, my love of nature and animals, or simply writing about more recent memories recalled from experiences of life, work, and marriage. It was through my writing that I began to understand that it was those life experiences that collectively helped shaped my life and give it true meaning.

Some of the stories I have written are humorous, some are serious, and some are simply informative, but all of them have come straight from my heart. I have written them in hopes of eliciting a small chuckle, a knowing smile, to spark a happy memory or to simply touch a warm place in the heart of the reader.

As my collection of writings began to grow, I was encouraged by many to put them together and publish a book.

And that is exactly what I did.

The following is a treasured collection of stories and memories of experiences that have brought meaning and purpose to my life. They are stories about living an ordinary life filled with extraordinary blessings.

They are stories about this, that, but mostly the other.

I hope you enjoy reading them, as much as I have enjoyed writing them. My greatest wish is that this book will spark a treasured memory for you and allow a moment of quiet reflection on the extraordinary blessings in your own life.

Growing Up Fifties Style

My two brothers and I were all born in the 1950s during the month of June, three years apart. My mother always joked it had something to do with those chilly October nights. I never really understood what she meant until much later in my life.

I was the only daughter and the middle sibling.

My father began his career as an attorney in a small local law firm in Fayetteville, North Carolina, the city where we lived. Later, he would be elected and serve as a local district court judge for twenty-seven consecutive years until he retired. Daddy as we called him, was a wise, well-respected, handsome man, who taught his children primarily through his example.

My mother passed away when I was just thirty-two years of age. I remember her as the most beautiful woman in the world. Mama had thick brown hair, sparkling blue eyes, and soft gentle hands. Mama was a stay-at-home mom with a quick wit, a kind heart, and a gentle spirit who always did more for others than for herself.

She was also quite the cook and entertainer.

Perhaps that is why I developed my love for the same.

All in all, I grew up in what I believe were the best of times. It was a time when you could sleep on warm evenings with the front door and windows wide-open and just the screen door latched, feeling perfectly safe. It was a time when parents sent their children outdoors to play without worry, knowing all the adults in the neighborhood were always watching out for all the kids, not just their own.

It was a time when life had a much slower pace and things were fairly simple.

As children, boundaries were set and rules were clear. We were expected to behave in public, respect our elders, and to never talk back to our parents. Talking back to your parents was called "sassing" and doing so could land you in a whole heap of trouble. The worst punishment of all, however, was simply a look of disapproval from a loving parent.

School and education were important.

We were told it was our job to attend on a regular basis, listen to our teachers, stay out of trouble, and make good grades. My parents took an active role in our education. My dad served as the elementary Parent Teacher Association president every year for twelve consecutive years. That was how long it took to get all three of us Carter kids through elementary school.

Each year, my mom served as something the school called a "Grade Mother." She helped out with school parties, activities, the annual Halloween carnival, and such.

It was not unusual to see either of my parents at school on any given day.

Up until five years of age, I lived in a small, white wooden frame house on a quiet tree-lined street in town. My memories of that time take me back to a fenced backyard, chinaberry trees that were perfect for climbing, Mr. Jolly in his musical ice cream truck on summer afternoons, and friendly neighbors who frequently visited our home for coffee and conversation.

We always had an assortment of pets to include dogs, a cat, a white duck named Dan, several hamsters, and a parakeet named Pete. Our parents taught us that it was important to be gentle and kind to our animals. They called them helpless creatures that depended on people to protect and care for them.

At the age of five, my family and I would move from this small home to a new, larger brick home about four miles away in the same city. This is where I would live until adulthood.

Our new home was located on a cul-de-sac, although I don't ever recall anyone ever using that word. That part of the street, where the neighborhood kids would congregate for games and conversation, was always referred to as "the Circle."

Our new house was built on a double lot bordered by a small creek and woods filled with tall pine trees. The lot was large enough for my dad, who was always a country boy at heart, to build a small fishing pond fed by underground springs.

The woods were thick and perfect for cutting paths and building forts. The nearby creek was shallow and proved to be a popular spot for wading and catching tadpoles in the summertime.

The banks of the creek were lined with a slick grayish clay substance. We used the clay to make homemade pottery, such as small ashtrays or little birds' nests with tiny balls placed inside for the eggs.

There was no public kindergarten; however, an Episcopal Church just up the street had begun a private kindergarten program. Somehow my parents managed to get me enrolled, even though I was technically a Southern Baptist.

From the very first day, I developed a love for kindergarten. Later I felt the same about elementary school, junior high, and high school. I loved my teachers and I enjoyed my friends. According to my report cards, I did fairly well academically and socially, with only an occasional reminder that I had a propensity to be a little talkative in class.

Church was a very important part of our lives. My dad was a deacon at Massey Hill Baptist Church where we attended each Sunday. My mom enjoyed hosting social events for members of their Sunday school class, and we always looked forward to Vacation Bible School in the summertime.

I also recall attending some old-fashioned down-home tent revivals from time to time, whenever they would come to town.

As far as recreation, my mom enrolled us in anything she could. She said it would help us develop into "well-rounded" individuals.

I took piano lessons, gymnastic class, and drama lessons, and I sang in a community children's choir. My brothers participated in different types of sports programs. My older brother, who showed talent in the area, took art lessons. My younger brother, much to his chagrin, was enrolled for a brief period of time in piano lessons.

My mom said she didn't ever want him to say he wasn't given the opportunity.

When we weren't in school or involved in planned recreational activities, my brothers and I just wanted to be outdoors. We would roam the woods, ride bikes, and play organized games with the other kids who lived in the neighborhood. Sometimes we would invent new games and develop a set of rules, spurred totally by imagination. It was not unusual for us to be outdoors until we were reluctantly called in for supper.

The parents in the neighborhood had different signals to get their children rounded up in the evening. One neighbor, a rather heavyset mom of five girls, would put two fingers in her mouth and let out a whistle so shrill I was sure you could hear in a neighboring county.

Another neighbor would flash the front porch lights on and off.

Our parents told us to be inside directly after the streetlights flickered on, which was around dusk. We ate our meals together as a family, with each of us having our own special seat at the kitchen table. Each weekday evening, supper was followed by homework, one television show, a bath, and then bed.

It was indeed a happy and a simple time in life.

Looking back, I know how blessed I was to have grown up in the best of times, embraced by the love and guidance of caring parents who believed in their children and taught us to believe that we had the ability to become whatever we chose to be.

After graduating from high school, I would go on to college, beginning as a music major and ending up as an education major.

I would graduate, get a job teaching first grade, working during the day and continuing my education in evenings. I would go on to become a school principal, followed by a brief stint working in Cincinnati as professional staff developer, and then finally venture out into the world as an independent educational consultant, all the while enjoying life as a single, professional female.

Then, during the summer of 2001, everything changed.

I met Mike.

Mike lived just outside Fayetteville in a small community known as Hope Mills, North Carolina. I was familiar with Hope Mills because I had relatives who lived there. In fact, my grandfather served as the police chief in Hope Mills in 1937.

Mike was the oldest of five siblings. His father was an Army Special Forces soldier who was seriously wounded at the beginning of the Vietnam War Conflict. He overcame his horrific injuries and medical problems to become a successful and respected real estate builder and developer in Hope Mills.

Mike's mother was a full-time stay-at-home mom.

From all accounts, our childhood paralleled in many ways, rooted in a love of nature and outdoors, beloved pets, and the ultimate importance of family, faith, community, and friendship.

Mike was one year my senior. Like me, he had never married.

He also seemed quite content being independent and living the life of a bachelor. His home—that he and his father designed and built—resembled a quaint cabin. Befitting, I thought, considering his love for hunting and fishing.

After four months of courtship, Mike and I were married in January 2002 on New Year's Day. The ceremony took place in a small quaint chapel in Las Vegas, Nevada.

Not long after we were married, Mike and I moved to the little town of Hope Mills to begin our life together.

Much like my dad, Mike is a country boy at heart. He is creative, has a quick wit and endearing sense of humor. He also is not one to hold back on what he is thinking.

Hope Mills Visitor

My friend from Cincinnati called me the other day.

"So how's life in Mayberry?" she asked.

That is what she calls Hope Mills, North Carolina, the small town where my husband Mike and I live. She calls it Mayberry because she says it reminds her of the fictitious southern town depicted in the classic television show Andy Griffith. She also references the blue and white sign on Main Street which reads "As Close to Mayberry as You're Gonna Get."

It is always interesting to get the perspective of someone else about our little community, especially someone like my friend who has lived most of her life in a large urban city with tall skyscrapers, swanky restaurants, corporate offices, and national sports teams.

I remember the first time my friend came to visit. For her first experience, my husband Mike and I decided to take her to Becky's Cafe for breakfast.

Becky's was as crowded as usual. The round stools at the counter were filled with customers, and there was only one open table remaining in the tiny restaurant.

We quickly claimed it as our own.

My friend picked up the menu and began to look at the breakfast selections.

Our waitress, Martha, was her usual friendly self.

"I will have the usual, Martha, with a glass of milk," Mike said.

"Me too," I said. "Only I will have a cup of coffee with mine."

"Do you both want your eggs on top of your grits?" Martha asked, as she scribbled on her order pad.

"Yes," we said, in harmony.

My friend needed a little more time to check out the menu so Martha left for a minute and then returned with my husband's glass of milk and my cup of coffee.

My friend was ready to place her order.

"I think I'll have the pancakes with a glass of milk," she said.

"Sorry, but we have just run out of milk," Martha replied.

"You have run out of milk?" my friend asked, almost in disbelief.

"Yes." Martha laughed. Then she pointed to Mike and said, "He got the last of it."

Mike joked, "You have to really be quick to live here in Hope Mills.

"So what do you want to do next?" I asked my friend as we were finishing up breakfast. "Do you want to take the boat down to the lake and go crappie fishing?"

At first, she was hesitant because of her fear of the water. However, we strapped her into a life vest and assured her she would be safe.

We spent a few hours puttering around Hope Mills Lake, fishing for crappie and just having a good time. She was amazed at how large the lake actually was when we turned the bend and ventured into the back area not visible from Main Street.

Late in the afternoon, after a little break, Mike asked my friend, "Have you ever shot a shotgun?"

"Are you kidding?" she gasped. "I've never touched a gun in my life!"

"Then come on!" my husband said. "You'll love this."

We jumped in his old pickup and took a ride through the countryside to a farm in a nearby community called Gray's Creek. With a little instruction from my husband, my friend successfully shot a few gourds off a vine.

"This is really fun!" she said.

On the way back home, my friend reminisced about how great it felt to be outside in the fresh air that day. She talked about the down-to-earth, friendly nature of the people she had met, how peaceful our small community was, and how wonderful it must be to live in a community where you could fish in your own special lake.

She talked about how much fun it was to go out into the country and to shoot a shotgun.

Everyday things that we took for granted, she found wonderful.

Walking toward the house late that evening, my friend spotted something on the sidewalk. It moved and she screamed.

"Relax. It's only a bullfrog," I said.

"If it's only a frog, then why is the thing so huge?"

"Because it's a Hope Mills bullfrog," I told her. "We grow them big here in Hope Mills."

The morning before she left for the airport, we had leftover barbeque ribs and collard greens for breakfast. That's when my friend told me that when she retires, she wants to move to Hope Mills.

She said, "You know, I think I would really like living in Mayberry."

And I think she would too.

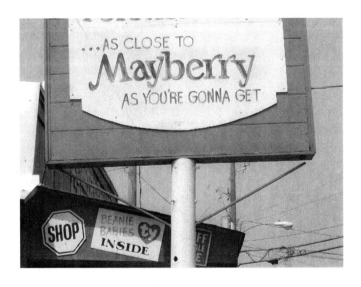

I'm a Teacher

What do you want to be when you grow up? I remember my kindergarten teacher, Mrs. Grace Hicks, asking my class that question one day. One by one, the children stood, faced the class, and boasted proudly about their future careers.

I remember there were some kids that were going to be doctors, some wanted to be firefighters, and some police officers. Others dreamed of being lawyers and some teachers like Mrs. Hicks. There were also those who had hopes of becoming nurses, a few soldiers; and there were one or two future truck drivers. When it came my turn, I stood and announced to the class that I planned to grow up and become a movie star! It must have really tickled Mrs. Hicks because that evening, she called my home to warn my parents about my Hollywood ambitions.

Needless to say, my dream to become a movie star was never fully realized. To this date, an occasional television interview and video web conferencing is as close as I have come. In fact, as with most people, what I planned to become when I grew up changed several times throughout my life. One thing for sure, however, it was those teachers like Mrs. Grace Hicks that had a tremendous impact on my life and on what I have become today.

Attending kindergarten at the age of five marked the beginning of my formal schooling experience. That was unusual because back in those days, there were no public kindergartens. I consider myself fortunate to have been given the opportunity.

I attended a private kindergarten sponsored by a nearby local church. It was an Episcopal Church, and we were a Southern Baptist family but that really didn't seem to matter all that much.

Once a week, the students would attend a little church service with the teacher. The only thing that I recall we did during that service, that we didn't do at my own church, was to light candles. I actually thought that was fun and wished we did it at our church. What I enjoyed most was when it came to be my turn to snuff out the flames of the candles with a brass candle snuffer.

The church which housed the kindergarten was located just up the street from my home. So each morning, I would walk to school with my best friend, June. We would spend a half day there, five days a week. The school day consisted of singing songs, playing games, painting pictures, listening to stories, learning to read, and sharing toys.

My favorite activity was show and tell, where we could bring something special from home to share with the class. We had a class mascot, a beige-colored hamster named Midget, who took turns going home with each of us on weekends. On Mondays, there would always be a report on Midget's antics, given by the person lucky enough to have her in their home for the weekend.

Each day, there was time spent playing outdoors in the fresh air. We had our favorite games that we requested to play more often than others. My favorite game was called "Whose Afraid of the Big Bad Wolf?" Mrs. Hicks, or her assistant, would always be the Big Bad Wolf and they would chase all of us little "piggies" around the playground. Funny, how even though they were much bigger and faster, they were never able to catch us.

On really cold days, when we would come inside from our play, Mrs. Hicks would kneel down and let us take turns putting our tiny hands into her thick hair, holding them against her head in order to warm them up. We had Ritz crackers and fruit juice for a snack and then would rest for a while on our little floor mats.

On holidays and special occasions, Mrs. Hicks would always make sure we had a gift to take home for our parents. During art time, we would make a cast of our small hands in plaster and dip jars into paint to create beautiful vases for Mother's Day presents.

We would plant beans in Dixie cups filled with dirt, place the cups in a window, water them each day, and watch the beans grow into plants. Finally, at the end of the year, we had a graduation ceremony and we hugged each other good-bye.

After kindergarten, other teachers began to take Mrs. Hicks's place—teachers like Mrs. Etta Cameron, Mrs. Becky White, Mrs. Edith Arnie, Mrs. Sally Allen, Ms. Carleen Moulder, and Mrs. Ruth Aderholt. Each teacher, in their own special way, made a lasting impression on me. They made school enjoyable and they made learning fun.

As I grew older, I eventually began to rethink my life ambition. Perhaps I too could become a teacher and help children learn, have fun, and enjoy coming to school. Maybe I could make a difference in their young lives, just like my own teachers did for me.

Eventually, I went on to realize my dream of becoming a teacher. And today, I am honored to be in a position to help other teachers as they work to become the very best teachers they can be.

I always take time to remind each teacher of the tremendous influence they have on the lives of the children they teach. I remind them of the importance of their work and that they really do touch the future and therefore change the world.

I often wonder whether Mrs. Grace Hicks would be surprised that, after all these years, I still remember all the important things I did and learned when I was in her kindergarten class.

For some reason, I think she probably would.

I think we can all remember those special teachers who made such a difference in our lives and helped us to become who we are today. So, as the bumper sticker I once read so amply put it, if you can read this, thank a teacher!

Lisa Waring

I Married a Hunter

I am not really sure what motivates a person to crawl out of a warm bed at 4:00 a.m. on a frosty morning to go deer hunting. For that matter, why would anyone walk miles through the woods in the dark, climb up a fifteen-foot ladder and sit alone in a tree for hours?

But for the deer hunter, I understand this is all considered part of the fun.

Over the years, I have made it a point to learn more about this sport my husband Mike finds so fascinating. Along with reading an occasional hunting magazine, I have tried watching those hunting shows on Saturday mornings. But for the most part, I find they are always the same—a couple of guys sitting in a tree stand whispering to each other for twenty-seven minutes, minus the time allotted for gun and ammo commercials.

Finally, during the last three minutes of the show, one of the hunters takes a shot and bags a trophy buck. Out of breath, they each talk about how much fun it was and how they will surely come back to that particular ranch or farm to hunt again next year.

The number of trips to deer-brought-home ratio at my house tells me, like most things you see on TV, those Saturday morning hunting shows are not necessarily how it works in real life.

I think the closest I've come to learning about deer hunting was seven years ago when I asked Mike if I could go with him and experience one of his trips. He was going to be hunting at a friend's farm in York, South Carolina. Instead of shooting with a rifle, the plan was for me to shoot nature pictures with my camera from a tree stand in the woods.

The drive to South Carolina was fun. After we arrived at the farm and settled in, my husband wanted to show me the place in the woods where I would be stationed with my camera the following morning.

We walked for what seemed like miles through briars and brush. I was totally lost because the scenery never seemed to change but Mike must have known exactly where he was going because we ended up at a metal tree stand out in the middle of nowhere.

"Just so you will know, we call this 'The Highway Patrolman' stand," he said proudly. "This is where you will be positioned tomorrow morning with your camera. I will be over there about two hundred yards in the 'Double Cedar' stand." He pointed through the woods.

At first I thought he was joking but he was serious.

All the tree stands had names and he knew where each one of them was located.

I still say the "Highway Patrolman" stand was forty feet tall but he declares it was only fifteen.

In order to practice, Mike suggested that I try climbing up the ladder and getting into the seat. Reluctantly, I slowly made my ascent to the top of the ladder. That was the easy part. Turning around in midair without something to hold on to was the hard part. I finally managed to do it, but don't ask me how. Then, facing forward, I somehow pulled myself up and backwards onto an old plastic pillow that I suppose was the seat.

Immediately, I looked around for a seat belt. There was none. However, I did see a long metal bar, like the one you have on the rides at the fair. That must be it, I thought to myself. I tugged on it but it wouldn't budge.

"That is the gun rest!" Mike yelled. "You use that bar to steady your rifle."

"So what keeps you from falling out of this thing?"

"You sit very still," he said. Then he smiled and reminded me that I would have to perform this mid-air maneuver all over again in the morning with a camera in my hand.

Eventually, after much coaxing, I did manage to climb back down the ladder of the tree stand. On the way back to the farmhouse, I was asked to practice walking lightly to avoid crunching tree limbs and branches.

And of course, there was this barbed-wire fence I had to practice crossing.

At dinner that evening, Mike informed me that we would need to be up and at our stands at 5:00 a.m.

"You mean you expect me to climb up in that tree stand and turn around with a camera in my hand in the dark?" I exclaimed. "Can I use a flashlight?"

"Nope," he said. "You might scare away the deer."

"Well, happy hunting," I replied. "Tomorrow I will be staying right here waiting for you to get back."

And that was the end of that.

I don't go hunting with Mike anymore. In fact, after that trip, I never asked to go hunting with him again.

And I have a sneaking suspicion that somehow that may have been the plan all along.

Part I

On Family

THE TIES THAT BIND

A Yellow Jaguar Bike

Life is always presenting us with golden opportunities to teach our children important lessons. These opportunities are often embedded in very simple everyday events. It is important that we look for these opportunities, seize them whenever they arise, and use them well.

I learned an important life lesson when I was around twelve years of age. It involved a bright yellow ten-speed bike displayed in the window of Hawley's Bicycle Shop. It thought it was absolutely the best-looking bike I had ever laid eyes on. The brand name was "Jaguar" and it was written on the side of the bike in slanted black letters.

It had horn-shaped handlebars that curved downwards, a slick black leather seat and thin, sturdy wheels like a racing bike.

I stared in the store window and knew that I wanted that bike in the worst kind of way. I could just visualize myself flying down the hill in our neighborhood on this yellow dream bike. I went inside the store and looked at the price tag. When I saw that it cost $100, my heart sank. It might as well have cost one million dollars.

In that day, a hundred dollars was a whole lot of money for a bicycle. I told my dad how much I wanted that yellow Jaguar, secretly hoping that he would offer to buy it for me. Of course, he didn't. However, he told me that if I wanted it that badly, I needed to develop a plan to earn the money and save it for the bike.

So I did just that. I went home determined to earn $100. I babysat kids in the neighborhood for fifty cents an hour. I did odd jobs around the house, and I squirreled away birthday money. Other opportunities to spend the money would arise, but I would try to stay focused on my mental picture of the bike, with me on the leather seat, flying down the neighborhood hill.

It took me almost a year, but I finally saved enough money to purchase the bike. With my little leather wallet in hand, I returned to Hawley's Bicycle Shop. I went in the store and took my money up to the counter. I told Mr. Hawley, the owner, I was there to buy the yellow Jaguar ten-speed and I had $100 to pay for it. I began taking the money out of my little wallet and putting it on the counter.

Mr. Hawley looked at me, smiled, and told me to put my money away. "The bike was already paid for months ago," he said, and they were already loading it in the backseat of my father's car.

I was puzzled.

I had worked almost a year to save up for this bike and then, out of the blue, my dad had decided to pay for it himself. On the way home, I asked my father why he told me to work and save money for the bike when he had planned to pay for it all along.

"You needed to know how badly you actually wanted it," he said. "You were willing to work hard towards a goal and you saved for something you wanted badly. I am proud of you."

I was now the proud owner of a new bright yellow ten-speed Jaguar bike.

For years, I never truly understood what my father did, but later in life I came to understand it. He was taking an opportunity to teach me something—a simple life lesson. My dad could have easily given me the money or just bought that bike for me on my first visit to Mr. Hawley's store. However, an opportunity presented itself to teach me something about the way life actually works. If you want something badly enough, you can earn it through hard work and effort.

Now that might not seem like such a big deal, but it taught me a huge lesson that has remained with me throughout my life. It helped shaped my value system and made me who I am today. Every day, opportunities like the one my dad encountered in the bicycle shop, present themselves to help us teach our children life lessons—like the importance of hard work, saving for a rainy day, the importance of perseverance and planning for future events.

By the way, at the suggestion of my father, I deposited that $100. I earned into my college fund.

The Preacher's Visit

This past weekend, Mike and I began our annual ritual of fertilizing the flowers and shrubs in our yard. Our gardening supplies included two bright yellow bags of cow manure, used primarily for the gardenias.

"Did I ever tell you about the time the preacher and his wife came to our house for Sunday dinner?" I asked Mike, as he popped opened the bag of manure with the blade of his shovel.

"The one about the preacher and the cow manure?" he asked, lifting the bag and pouring its contents into the bucket.

"Yeah, that one," I said.

"Yes, you did, several times." He chuckled. "But go ahead and tell me again."

You see, he knows that it is one of those family stories that get told over and over again. You never get tired of telling it and you still laugh like it was the first time you heard it.

When I was growing up, our family attended Massey Hill Baptist Church. For most of those years, our preacher was the Reverend D. H. Lowder. Both he and his wife were very well-liked and respected by the congregation. Often, members of the church family would invite the Lowders to their home for Sunday dinner. Everyone looked forward to their turn to host the popular minister and his wife. Needless to say, everyone was also looking to make a good impression.

I was fairly young at the time the Lowders were invited to have Sunday dinner with us. We had just moved into our new house and my mom, who really liked to entertain, worked hard to prepare, and planned for every little thing—the meal, the linen table cloth and napkins, the fine china, the good crystal, and the silverware.

Very late on Saturday afternoon, as she was busy working on the last details for the Sunday guests, she heard a noise and looked out the window. To her horror, she saw a huge dump truck, depositing a full load of fresh cow manure all over our front lawn. This was not the packaged, processed kind you get in the bright yellow bags today; this was the real deal brought straight to our house directly from a local farm.

To this day, I am not sure who was at fault here, but there was definitely some mix-up in communication. My dad says he knew the minister and his wife were scheduled to visit. But he says he did not realize it was on that particular Sunday. Of course, once the smelly fertilizer was dumped all over the yard, there was obviously no getting it loaded back on the truck.

As the story goes, the dinner was planned and it was too late to turn back. To resolve the problem of having to walk through the manure-filled yard, my dad placed long wooden planks, end to end, between the road and the front porch.

The following day, you can only imagine how my mom must have felt watching out the window as Preacher Lowder and his wife dressed in her Sunday best, made their way single file down the wooden planks toward the front door of our home, using their arms to steady themselves and to keep from stepping off either side into the manure-filled yard.

Following some profuse apologies, it turned out to be a wonderful visit for everyone. The yard became the source of some joking and laughter, too. And years later, we still talk about the day Preacher Lowder and his lovely wife joined us for Sunday dinner.

So I guess the moral of this story is, just when you think you have everything planned, someone can still come by and dump a truckload of cow manure in your front yard.

Don't let it get you down and continue on.

Most of the time, you will look back on it later and laugh.

Chinese Checkers

I was recently going through a closet that held several sacred keepsakes from my childhood and ran across an old Chinese checkerboard. I had not seen the flat, round tin container, decorated with dragons and filled with small marbles for decades.

My mind immediately drifted back to another time. I thought about my great-aunt Ethel and all the Chinese checker games we played together when I was a child.

Aunt Ethel was my maternal grandfather's sister who lived in White Oak, North Carolina. She had a small frame, twinkling eyes, a magnetic personality, and quite the reputation for her skill at playing the game of Chinese checkers.

No one could beat her, although many tried.

Be it an adult or a kid, the final jump of the marble into the little triangle on the board was always hers.

And when she won, she would stare you straight in the eyes and grin at you in triumph.

Aunt Ethel would occasionally come "to town" to visit with us. I always looked forward to spending time with her.

She said she went to bed with the chickens and got up with the chickens.

So we would all go to bed early when Aunt Ethel visited. The next morning, we would be up at the crack of dawn, ready to start the day.

Sometimes, I would go to her home to spend weekends with her.

Those are my most special memories.

Aunt Ethel lived in the country in an old, wooden two-story house with exposed rafters on the second floor.

The boards on the house were a weathered gray.

She had a porch that stretched the full length across the front of the house.

There was an indoor hand pump for water in her kitchen and an old clawfoot bathtub in an unheated bathroom. Her telephone was connected to a party line with her neighbors.

There were always bags of blueberries from the season in her chest freezer, which was in the hallway.

At night, we slept together in a big feather bed in the front room, warmed by a wood-burning stove.

In the early evening, Aunt Ethel and I would sit on a swing on her front porch after supper, swinging, listening to the crickets, and watching the lightning bugs.

Sometimes she would tell me stories about when she was a little girl.

Then, we would go inside and she would bring out her Chinese checkerboard.

I didn't understand the strategy behind the game. So I mostly remember randomly jumping my marbles to any open slot and in no particular order.

Aunt Ethel would watch and stay very quiet. She would always smile before slowly making her jump.

Every game, she always, always managed to make the final jump. She would fill her triangle with the little marbles to be declared the winner.

I never remember feeling bad or angry for not winning.

I only remember looking forward to playing with her again.

Aunt Ethel told me that if you got sand in your shoes in White Oak, it meant you would always come back. On Sunday afternoon, before my parents came to pick me up from my visit, I would always go out in her yard and put sand in my shoes.

I wanted to make sure I would always come back to White Oak to visit with my Aunt Ethel.

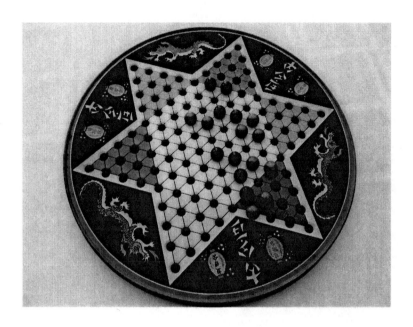

Proud to be a GRIT

I saw a T-shirt in a store window the other day. It was pink and on the front of the shirt, there were penciled profiles of some ladies wearing wide-brimmed hats. The caption beneath the picture read, "GRITS, Girls Raised in the South." I guess that makes me a GRIT.

When traveling to other parts of the country, people quickly recognize that fact. They say my southern accent gives me away, although I can't really hear an accent myself. I have been told that I make a one-syllable word, like dog, sound like a three-syllable word.

I usually just smile and tell them that from my perspective, they are the ones with the accent.

People also tell me they can recognize my southern roots through my strange vocabulary as well. I use words like young'uns when I am talking about children, or fixin' when I am fixin' to go somewhere. And I refer to my diet Pepsi as a drink, instead of a pop or soda. Some find those southern idiosyncrasies rather charming. Sometimes they even ask me what other unusual words are in my vocabulary.

Once, while traveling out west, I was asked to say my vowels for a group of people which, in turn, attempted to repeat them back to me mimicking my southern drawl. We all laughed. "Surely," I said. "I don't sound like that!"

I consider being raised in the south as something special. I learned a lot of things growing up southern. I learned important things that are an integral part of our culture and our southern way of life.

I learned that tea is sweet, unless you ask otherwise, and that turnips, collards, and grits all taste good, if they were cooked right.

I learned it is important to respect my elders.

You should always say "Yes, ma'am" and "No, sir" to your elders, simply out of respect for their age.

You should listen to them because they have the wisdom of years.

I learned that the words "please" and "thank you" will get you far in life and that sometimes it is okay to tell a little white lie, if it keeps from hurting other people's feelings.

I learned that if you are invited to someone's home for a meal, you should always try your best to clean your plate, even if you are full or don't particularly like the food that they serve.

And when the meal is over, you take your dinner plate to the kitchen and offer to help wash dishes, even if you know they really don't want you to.

I learned that if a relative, friend, or neighbor is sick, you take food to their house and then call them from time to time to check on them until they are feeling better.

You tell them you are sorry that they are "under the weather," no matter how serious the illness.

And when someone passes away, you take food to their house and you sit with their family and loved ones, even if no one feels much like talking.

I learned that to have a good friend one must be a good friend and to have a good neighbor one must be a good neighbor.

I learned that school is important, education is important, and that teachers are to be respected.

I learned that whether you are a ditch digger or the president of the United States, it is important to do the very best job you can because any job worth doing is worth doing well.

I learned that if you are lucky enough to climb the ladder of success, you should avoid stepping on other people's toes and fingers on the way up. You will also meet those same people again on your way back down.

I learned that those things that go around usually come back around, if you wait long enough.

I learned that blood runs thicker than water and when all is said and done, in the end all you will have left is your family.

I learned that common sense is not always that common.

I learned that everyone is important and has a place on this earth, and that it is our responsibility to look out for those that are less fortunate.

I learned to respect the environment and to take care of animals because they are all God's creatures.

And growing up in Church, I learned that there is something much greater than me in charge of my life.

I really feel blessed that I had the opportunity to grow up in southeastern North Carolina.

I am proud that I continue to live here.

By the way, I did not purchase one of those pink T-shirts I saw in the store window that day.

You see, I don't really need a shirt to advertise that I am one of those GRITS. My southern accent will give me away every time.

Told Once,
and Then a Thousand Times

Last week, I settled into my window seat on the airplane and listened to the flight attendant as she began to make her routine safety announcements. She requested that we pay very close attention and listen as she reviewed and described important safety information concerning our aircraft. She also suggested that we follow along with her using a safety card that was located in the seatback pocket in front of us.

She held the card up in front of her for everyone to see. I looked around and noticed that no one on the plane was reaching for the safety card in their seatback pocket. In fact, it appeared that no one was paying much attention to the flight attendant at all. My guess is that most people had heard that same speech so many times they probably had it memorized like me. Nonetheless, the flight attendant continued on with her announcement as if everyone was paying attention. She talked about the smoke detectors in the lavatory, the emergency lighting on the floor, the exit row doors, and the use of the oxygen masks and the seat belts.

When she finally finished her safety speech, she began making her way through the cabin for her final check to make sure we were all buckled in. That is when the gentleman seated next to me leaned over and whispered, "She forgot to tell us not to run with scissors in our hands."

I laughed.

"Everyone is so safety conscious these days," he said. "Looking back, sometimes I wonder how people our age ever survived to become adults!"

I guess in some ways he is right. Back when I was growing up, things used to be a lot different. It really wasn't such a "childproof" world back then.

We rode our bicycles around the neighborhood without safety helmets on our heads for protection. We roller-skated without helmets or knee pads, too. There were no child-proof windows and locks on the doors of our car to keep us locked safely inside and prevent us from opening the window while the car was moving.

We rode in the backseat of our parent's car without seatbelts and children's car seats. Sometimes we even slept lying down in the back seat of the car and took turns crawling up on the back dashboard.

Aspirin bottles had caps that popped off easily with a simple flip of your thumb or twisted off with little or no effort. There were no child-proof caps. There were no special safety scissors made especially for children. The scissors in the house were full-sized adult scissors and we used them as kids on a regular basis.

There were no paragraph-long written warnings on container labels describing all the possible dangers associated with the product or the hazards of choking on small parts of toys. Most of our warnings, we got directly from our parents. And much like the safety announcement given by the flight attendant on my plane, we heard those same speeches many, many times. In fact, most of those speeches began the same way. "If I told you once, I told you a thousand times!"

I suppose it is somewhat amazing that so many of us did survive those years growing up in a not so childproof world. Maybe it was because we were lucky.

But I also believe it was because we had parents that watched out over us. They tried to keep us out of harm's way and they took the time to talk to us, even if it meant having to remind us over and over about things. They did their best to childproof our world and to keep us safe.

And we chose to listen and heed those loving speeches that we heard not once but a thousand times. We even had some of them memorized, although it may have appeared at the time that we were not paying much attention at all.

Dad's Old Report Card

I was recently going through some old papers and ran across a copy of one of my father's report cards. My father passed away on August 8, 2011, at the age of eighty-six.

He began first grade at Massey Hill School in 1930 and graduated in 1941. My dad loved school and he spoke often of his former teachers. He believed deeply in the power of a good education.

He was also the smartest man I have ever known.

I was curious to see what learning expectations were in place for students when my father was a seventh grade student. It appears to me, at least according to his report card, receiving a quality education at Massey Hill School was about much more than just learning the three Rs.

The 1937 report card was divided into two sections.

The first section of the report card addressed academic achievement and the second half dealt with character development and citizenship.

Academically, students received grades in seven subject areas—namely, reading, oral language, written language, social studies, arithmetic, music, and art.

In the area of reading, students were expected to get thoughts for themselves (silent reading), give thoughts to others (oral reading), get new words readily, read silently without pointing and moving lips, read rapidly, read in addition to assignments, and to appreciate good literature.

In oral language, students were expected to use correct speech, talk and ask questions intelligently, organize thoughts well, and to contribute to group discussion.

In the area of written language, students were expected to express thoughts clearly, arrange work legibly and neatly, organize thoughts well, spell words for their age group, and show evidence of creative thoughts in their writing.

In social studies, which included history and geography, students were expected to be able to secure needed information, use information to solve problems, reason from cause to effect, and to find and develop new interests.

In arithmetic, students were expected to know number facts for their age group, think through a problem, work rapidly, make few mistakes, and apply their knowledge to solve everyday problems.

In music, students were expected to enjoy good music, sing with the group, teach songs to others, and create their own music.

Finally, expectations in art were to appreciate works of others, gain knowledge of the arts, express ideas of others, and originate their own ideas.

Interestingly enough, the second section of the report card that addressed character development and citizenship was weighted just as heavily as the academic side. Obviously, the belief was that academics, character, and citizenship were all equally important in the development of a well-rounded student prepared to be successful in life.

Under citizenship and character, students received grades in six areas: Health and appearance, physical education, initiative and self-reliance, courtesy and consideration, honesty, obedience and self-control.

Under health and appearance, students were expected to keep clean skin, hair, nails, body, and clothes. They were also expected to maintain clean, well-repaired teeth, express good posture for possibilities, possess an abundance of energy and vitality, and to assist in preventing communicable diseases.

In physical education, students were expected to meet commonly set goals for their grade level.

Under initiative and self-reliance, students were expected to think and work independently, be resourceful in finding things to do, practice desirable leadership, and to cooperate in group activities.

In the area of courtesy and consideration, students were expected to take turns graciously, greet people pleasantly, laugh and talk quietly, observe courtesies practiced by a lady or gentleman, listen to others without interrupting, be prompt in meeting obligations, seek justice for all, and to be considerate of others.

In the area of obedience and self-control, students were expected to respond promptly and willingly to authority, refrain from making alibis, sulking and quarreling, submit gracefully to unavoidable misfortune, be orderly when the teacher is absent, and refrain from meddling in the affairs of others.

Lastly and my favorite, in the area of honesty, students were expected to admit mistakes and wrongdoings and to make amends, to refrain from cheating and misrepresentations, and to support candidates who are fitted for office.

After being in education for over three decades, it was interesting for me to reflect on what was expected from my dad's generation, often referred to as the greatest generation, when they were students in school. Discovering that it was an equal balance between academic achievement, strong character development and citizenship did not surprise me at all.

Imaginary Family Names

It would appear that my great-niece Jordynn has inherited my vivid imagination. She is two and a half years old. The other day, I was talking with my sister-in-law Rebecca, Jordynn's grandmother, on the phone and could hear her chattering away in the background.

I asked Rebecca if I could speak with her.

She handed Jordynn the phone and I heard her little voice utter a familiar "Hey, Yisa!"

Since she has a little trouble with her Ls, that's what she calls me. I gave my usual response, "Hey, Jordynn. What are you doing?"

The toddler, who is never short for words, gave a lengthy reply. Much of what she said was indiscernible excited garble but I did manage to catch the word "Cinderella." She handed the phone back to my sister-in-law and I asked if Jordynn was looking at a book or watching a show about Cinderella on TV.

"Oh no, I am Cinderella," Rebecca said. "That's my new name."

It turns out that Jordynn has assigned everyone in the family a new name.

No one knows why, she just started doing it. "Around here, we all answer to our new names, not our real names," Rebecca said. According to Jordynn, her grandmother is "Cinderella" and her grandfather is "Prince." Her mother is "Mermaid" and her baby sister, Madilynn, "Froggy."

"Why Froggy?" I asked, somewhat bemused. That was when I was informed that Jordynn had named herself "Princess." Froggy has something to do with the "The Princess and the Frog," my sister-in-law told me. Luckily, baby Madilynn is still too young to understand all this.

Anyway, I couldn't resist asking Jordynn if I also had a new name.

She returned to the phone and answered my question without any hesitation. "You are Booty," she said in a very matter-of-fact way. "Booty?" I asked. "Yes, Booty "You know, like Booty and the Beast."

"So if I am Booty, does that mean your uncle Mike is the Beast?" I chuckled.

"Yeah," Jordynn said, and then she handed the phone back to Cinderella so she could return to watching Yo Gabba Gabba on TV.

After I hung up, I couldn't resist calling my aunt Joyce.

She always enjoys hearing about Jordynn's antics. I explained to her that if she wanted to find out her new name, she should contact Jordynn. I joked with her not to wait too long because she might run out of the good names.

What I didn't tell Aunt Joyce is that I had already gotten wind that her name could now possibly be "Arial."

Curiosity got the best of Aunt Joyce.

She called Jordynn right after speaking with me to inquire about a new name.

Turns out Aunt Joyce isn't Arial after all. Jordynn informed her that she was now "Belle."

She was "Aunt Joyce Belle" to be exact.

Of course, all this prompted me to e-mail my cousin Lela. I asked her if she wanted to know her new name according to Jordynn. She e-mailed me back that she wasn't really interested because she wanted the name Booty and it would appear that Booty was already taken. I responded back that if she was lucky, her new name might be "Booty" too.

But then of course, it could also be "SpongeBob SquarePants."

Still waiting to hear back.

Beyond Coincidence

My brother called on a Sunday afternoon. He and his wife were in a restaurant having lunch with a group of friends from their church. The group had been plotting a joke to play on one of their friends. It turns out the victim's name was Warren Dunshee who attends the same church.

He owns and operates a vehicle escort service.

The service assists in the safe transport of oversized vehicles, such as mobile homes, heavy machinery and large equipment on roads and highways. My brother asked me to call Warren and leave a message on his answering machine because being a stranger, he would not recognize my voice. My instructions were to say that I had recently seen the company sign for Dunshee's Escort Service and that I was calling to inquire about an escort for a party that I would be attending on Friday night.

I couldn't resist, so I went along with the joke, made the call, and left the message. Warren returned my call later that evening, somewhat embarrassed.

He left a message on our answering machine, politely explaining that he didn't run that particular kind of escort service. He said he would not be able to help me with my date for Friday evening and he wished me luck.

Then the joke backfired as I found myself having to explain the message left on my machine which was retrieved by my husband!

When the dust settled, everyone laughed.

Sometime later, I met Warren at a birthday party given for my dad and he mentioned the practical joke. We both laughed again.

Then he told me that he had noticed the name Waring on his caller ID the day I called.

"Are you any kin to Tommy Waring of Hope Mills?" he asked.

I told him, "Indeed, Tommy Waring is my husband's late father."

"Well, I'll be," he said. "Tommy and I served together in the military."

He went on to tell me that both he and Tommy were members of the same Special Forces team from Fort Bragg. "I was actually jumping with him the day he was injured," Warren told me. I thought to myself, *It really is a small world!*

Sadly, I never had the opportunity to meet Mike's father. He passed away January 8, 2001. However, my husband speaks of his father often. So when Warren told me about serving on the same Special Forces team with Tommy, and jumping with him the day he was injured, I knew what he was talking about for having listened to Mike's stories.

The two men were both a part of a Special Forces operation team based on the island of Okinawa. At that time, teams of Special Forces soldiers were being deployed to several Southeast Asian countries to secretly train and set the stage for what would soon become the Vietnam conflict. On August 27, 1960, Special Forces soldiers were making a water jump as part of their preparation and training in Okinawa. Tommy had parachuted out of his plane. Unknowingly, the tide had receded and the water where he landed was extremely shallow, only about two feet deep.

Tommy's parachute malfunctioned just before landing and his body crashed with full force into a coral reef hidden just beneath the surface of the shallow water.

A nearby rescue boat retrieved him from the water and he was immediately transported by helicopter to a hospital in Okinawa. His injuries were so severe that he was flown by plane to a much larger hospital just outside of Tokyo.

There he remained for three months, undergoing extensive surgeries.

Later, he was flown back to the states where he spent many more months in and out of Walter Reed Army Hospital as his body healed. Almost every bone in Tommy's body was shattered and broken. His injuries were so extensive that at first, doctors did not expect him to live, but he did.

Then they told him he would never walk again, but he did.

Not only did he live and walk, Tommy Waring returned to Hope Mills with his wife Betty Jean, raised five children, and went on to become a very successful land developer and business owner.

He established Pioneer Homes, a construction company which built over four hundred homes in the Hope Mills area and surrounding counties.

Ironically, Warren was preparing to jump from a second plane that was following behind Tommy's plane that fateful day in August. Upon viewing the incident with the plane ahead, Warren said his jumpmaster and his pilot made a quick decision to detour away from the shallow water and find deeper water so the soldiers on their plane could jump safely.

After hearing that amazing story, I asked Warren to join us for dinner.

I thought it might be nice for Mike to have a chance to talk to him. It was a very pleasant evening. Just before he left that night, Warren spoke serenely of the special bond that exists between servicemen and the great professionalism of the Special Forces team of which both he and Tommy were a part. He told me that after nearly half a century, he had a difficult time remembering Tommy's face.

However, as the evening progressed, he said he grew to recognize a certain familiarity in my Mike's face. Warren retired from Special Forces and settled in Parkton, North Carolina.

Forty-seven years later, Mike met a man who served his country with his father and who was there on the day that his father nearly met his death in a parachuting accident; perhaps, even someone whose life was saved because of his father's accident.

And to think that it all happened as a result of a practical joke and a caller ID.

Thanksgiving

Each holiday brings with it a golden opportunity to create precious memories that can last for a lifetime. Many of my own special memories are the ones that were created as a child spending each Thanksgiving Day at my grandmother Carter's home.

Opening the door, we were always greeted with a wonderful smell of food in the air. It wasn't one particular kind of food that smelled so delicious.

It was all kinds of food smells that were mingled together to create a wonderful aroma that became synonymous in my mind with Thanksgiving. After the hugs and hellos, my two brothers, three cousins, and I would play in the yard while the food finished cooking and the tables were being prepared.

Later, when it was time to eat, we were all called in to wash our hands and bow our heads in prayer before dinner. Thanksgiving prayer was always a little extra long so I would sometimes open one eye and peek to see if I could catch anyone else peeking. When the prayer was over, the kids would all be instructed to form a single file line in the kitchen. Under the watchful eyes of parents, one by one we would walk past the stove and countertop and fill our plates to the brim from the pots, pans, dishes, and platters.

All the food was delicious but I did have my favorites: Aunt Jean's sweet tea, fresh turnips, made-from-scratch biscuits, dressing and the gravy graced generously with giblets and sliced boiled eggs. My very favorite item was the lacy cornbread—a thin cornbread fried to a crisp in a cast iron skillet. I was told that it was called "lacy cornbread" because the edges were filled with little tiny holes that looked like lace. Smeared with butter, I thought lacy cornbread was food fit for a king.

Balancing our plates, the children would then be escorted to take our respective places at the kitchen table. We sat in wooden chairs at a little wooden table covered with a plastic table cloth. On the table, we did manage to get our own stick of butter, our own jar of molasses and salt and pepper shaker. We drank our sweet tea from plastic tumblers and old jelly jars with pictures of cartoon characters. And if I remember correctly, our plates didn't always match. Every now and then, a grown-up would appear in the doorway of the kitchen just to make sure we were all okay, no one was fighting, and that we were all eating our vegetables.

The dining room was the place where the grown-ups gathered to eat. The table in the dining room always sported a fancy linen table cloth, china plates and silverware. The grown-ups drank their sweet tea out of beautiful crystal goblets, made with etched glass. They were kept safely displayed in my grandmother's china cabinet throughout the year and only brought out for special occasions. I remember staring at them when I would visit and wonder what it would be like to drink my tea from something so elegant.

After the Thanksgiving meal, there were always three or four desserts from which to choose. We would quickly gobble down our choice, asked to be excused from the kitchen table, and return outside to play. Some of the grown-ups washed the dishes by hand and others sat in chairs and dozed off while sitting straight up.

When I was finally old enough, I was invited to sit at the dining room table at my grandmother's to eat my Thanksgiving meal off the fine china and drink my sweet tea from those fancy crystal goblets. Now, many years have come and gone.

My grandmother has passed away.

My aunt Jean still lives in my grandmother's house and she still makes the best sweet tea in the world. Whenever I visit for a meal, she always offers a seat at the dining room table. But

I always opt to sit at that little wooden kitchen table with the wooden kitchen chairs.

That is where my wonderful Thanksgiving memories from childhood were created.

Uncle Lentz

My Uncle Lentz always called me Lisa Ann. That isn't my real name and he knew it. My real name is Lisa Elaine. No matter, Uncle Lentz still called me Lisa Ann. I was never sure why he did that, but I never said anything about it because to tell you the truth, it always made me feel kind of special.

That was what was so endearing about Uncle Lentz. He could always make you feel special even if you had really not done anything out of the ordinary.

I think Uncle Lentz had a way of making everyone feel special like that.

Lentz Horner Carter was my dad's younger brother and his only brother. He was born in Grays Creek in October of 1928, graduated from Massey Hill High School in 1949, and settled down to live in Massey Hill, just down a narrow walking path from Grandmother's house.

To get to his house, you had to walk past the chicken coops, open the gate on the chain-linked fence, and then run like the devil to the back porch in order to escape a Jack Russell terrier or two that were usually nipping at your heels. I spent many a Sunday afternoon on that narrow walking path going from my grandmother's house to Uncle Lentz's house to visit.

Uncle Lentz was dearly loved by everyone in his family, including his wife Joyce, his only child Lela and her husband Mark. He was a handsome man and from pictures bore a great resemblance to my grandfather Carter, who passed away when I was only five years of age.

Uncle Lentz was a carpenter by trade and he was good at it.

He built a lot of houses, including his own.

A gifted comedian, Uncle Lentz had a way of saying the funniest things. He could tell stories that would make you laugh, sometimes so hard the tears rolled down your face.

I remember him telling a story about a country ham that had disappeared from his back porch and what he did in order to catch the thief. Anyone else would have told you that same story in a few sentences and that would have been the end of it. Not Uncle Lentz.

By the time he finished telling the story, I was totally in stitches and doubled over in laughter.

Uncle Lentz loved to fish. He enjoyed family get-togethers and a special green Jell-O salad that was named in his honor— Uncle Lentz Salad. I made sure I had it for him anytime he visited. He loved oyster roasts, drinking coffee with friends at Hardee's, and watching ballgames.

And he loved chickens.

In fact, every Christmas, I would spend hours in search of something that had to do with a chicken as a gift for Uncle Lentz.

This Christmas was no exception. I found a stuffed rooster that crowed when you pressed its belly and I said to myself, "Now I know Uncle Lentz will really like that!" This Christmas, however, Uncle Lentz was too sick to attend the annual family Christmas gathering which was held early in December. We all missed him in his red pants, red shirt, and red hat with "Miss Kitty's" written across the front of it. It was the first Christmas gathering that I think he ever missed.

I sent a large cup of Uncle Lentz Salad to the hospital, and they said he seemed really excited to get it but could only manage to eat a few bites. Uncle Lentz tried to eat it though, and I know he did it partly because it was good and partly because it was from me.

Uncle Lentz spent his last days here with us at the Village Green Nursing Care facility. It wasn't easy watching such a beloved and proud man become dependent on nursing care, but then he was very sick. There was a special person at the facility, a nurse by the name of Samuel. Samuel spent time caring for my uncle Lentz in his final days and in his final hours. Samuel treated my uncle with the compassion, dignity, and respect that he so very much deserved. I know that Samuel didn't really know Uncle Lentz—the carpenter, the comedian, the fisherman, the beloved brother, son, husband, father, friend, and uncle—who could so easily make everyone laugh and feel so very special. But Samuel must have known that he was all those things because that was the way he treated him.

My uncle Lentz passed away on that Christmas Day. His family was there with him to say good-bye. I can't say for sure, but I choose to believe he heard that rooster crowing when its belly was pressed that rainy afternoon. I saw it on his face.

He will be missed and he will very much be remembered. I believe everybody deserves to have an "Uncle Lentz" in their life—someone that makes them feel special when they really haven't done anything out of the ordinary at all.

The Oyster Roast

Last Sunday, a cold wind whipped through the trees and it rained, as the saying goes, just like cats and dogs. The weather forecast called for snow late in the evening. Probably the last thing most people would have thought about having that day was an outdoor event like an oyster roast. But when it comes to our family, especially the Carter side of the family, neither rain, nor sleet, nor threat of snow can keep us from eating oysters.

As a kid, I was taught that we could only eat oysters during months that are spelled with the letter r—which meant September through April. Our family oyster roasts always took place outdoors in our side yard. Steaming large pots of oysters, during what we called the "R" months, was always a special treat.

Later, oysters would slide their way into a special holiday tradition for our family. They became the featured ingredient in a dish served up on Christmas morning. Our family would also discover the joy of attending the annual Massey Hill Oyster Roast—considered by many to be an oyster lover's dream. Heck, my husband even decided to ask my dad for my hand in marriage over a bushel bag of steamed oysters.

So last Sunday, in celebration of my father's eighty-fourth birthday, we planned an old-fashioned oyster roast for the family. Of course, the plans were to have it as we usually do—outside in the yard.

The weather, however, refused to cooperate.

Once you have a couple of bushels of Carolina oysters sitting in your garage, there is really not much you can do except to go forward. So what was to be an outdoor oyster roast quickly had to be transformed into an indoor-outdoor event. As most people who attend them know, oyster roasts can be quite messy. They require lots of towels, more towels, oyster knives, gloves, and large buckets in which to pitch the shells.

That is one main reason I was a little hesitant about having eight people shuck bushels of steamed oysters in my kitchen. However, with a little thought and some planning, we developed a system and it worked like a charm.

First, the kitchen table itself had to be protected by several thick layers of plastic cloths. A bucket was then placed nearby for the empty shells. A disposable bowl for the melted butter and another for the cocktail sauce was placed on the table, along with a jar of horseradish, a bottle of catsup, and a container of tartar sauce. My sister-in-law usually mixes all the aforementioned ingredients together to make a concoction she calls her "special dipping sauce."

The oysters were steamed in large pots outside on the deck. An awning provided a small amount of shelter from the blowing rain. After they were steamed, a pot of oysters was brought inside and deposited into a large aluminum roasting pan on the kitchen table where those waiting patiently to eat them sat, clinching kitchen towels and oyster knives. In an instant, the sound of casual conversation in the room was replaced by loud clicking, cracking, and slurping noises. After a few minutes, those noises gradually subsided and conversation returned to the room. The bucket, filled with empty shells, was taken outside and dumped.

Another pot of oysters was brought into the kitchen and the process was repeated.

I noticed the ones that remained outdoors, who were actually doing all the work, did not seem bothered at all by the inclement weather. They stood huddled around the steaming pots—talking, laughing, shucking, and eating oysters themselves.

So despite the weather, it all worked out just fine. Our first ever indoor-outdoor oyster roast was deemed a success. In fact, by late afternoon, the only evidence of an oyster roast occurring that day was a large trash container filled with empty shells. With the exception of a few stray oysters on the floor, which our dog helped to clean up, even my kitchen was left in good order.

Life's Simple Pleasures

My dad was both a frugal and a wise man. He was always quite content to make use of whatever he had, as long as it still worked. My dad never asked for anything. He saved everything and he wasted nothing.

And what he had, he treated with good care. That made it especially difficult to buy gifts for him on special occasions.

Each year, at Christmas time, we spent hours trying to come up with something we thought he would not only like, but would also put to good use. One Christmas, I thought we had finally come up with three perfect gifts for my dad, three things that even he would admit he needed and would put to good use—a television, a Hope Mills ball cap, and an old coffee mug.

Even though my dad's old TV wasn't broken, the digital age would soon render it useless. According to my brother, even a conversion box wouldn't work on his older model television. So all his kids chipped in and bought dad a brand new, large flat screen TV. When he opened the box Christmas morning, he definitely appeared to be delighted and most appreciative.

My dad's favorite old light blue Hope Mills ball cap had worn with age. I suspected he would continue to wear it, but he did actually seem rather pleased with the new sportier navy and white one he received as the second gift.

But of all the gifts he received, I think my dad seemed the most tickled when he pulled the least expensive one out of an old recycled gift bag, a "Rise and Shine" Hardee's coffee mug. You see, Hardee's restaurant had a special promotion going where if you brought in one of the vintage tan and brown "Rise and Shine" coffee mugs, popular in the late 1980s, you could use the cup to get free coffee refills. My dad's old "Rise and Shine" mug was cracked from use and had developed a slow leak.

It took a lot of searching, but believe it or not, we did finally locate a 1986 Hardee's mug in mint condition for my dad. Since one of his favorite pastimes was enjoying coffee with his friends at Hardee's, he was quite thrilled to have his old leaky coffee mug replaced with another old mug in much better shape.

I believe my dad enjoyed his Christmas gifts that year. He also reminded us that it is not always necessary to have the newest or the latest everything in life, especially if we take good care of what we have and put it to use.

Thanks, Dad, for helping us all remember that it is often the simpler things in life that make us the most happy.

A Bell with Family Connections

An article entitled "Gives His Life to Ring Fire Alarm" was published in the Fayetteville Observer on June 4, 1921. It reads as follows:

> William McNeill, night watchman for the cotton mill factory of Hope Mills No. 2, six miles south of Fayetteville, lost his life while ringing a fire bell for the fire that destroyed the home occupied by L. H. Songer this morning about 2 o'clock.
>
> He died in Pittman Hospital in this city this morning.
>
> Mr. McNeill climbed up the belfry and was ringing the bell with all the power of his command when suddenly he was either struck by the swinging bell or lost his balance and tumbled out of the belfry to the ground, suffering a broken neck and crushed skull. He was rushed to Pittman Hospital, but there was no chance for him and he died shortly after reaching there. He was the son of Hector McNeill of Hope Mills, No. 2, and a man of a family.
>
> The Songer home, which was formerly the old Briggs place, was one of the oldest residences in the county. Practically all of its contents were destroyed in the fire. The cause of the fire is unknown.

This tattered article had been carefully clipped and tucked away inside an old McNeill family book, along with other significant articles and documentation about our family history.

William J. McNeill was my great-great-uncle Bill.

Reading the account documented in this old news article caused me to pause and think about this uncle I never knew. I tried to envision what he looked like and the tragic events that occurred in those early morning hours eighty-six years ago.

William J. McNeill had a niece, Eva McNeill Reynolds, who

continues to reside in the Gray's Creek community. Miss Eva turned one hundred on September 21, 2008. She was just a young girl at the time of Uncle Bill's death. She told me that most of what she remembers came from accounts of his accident that were given through family stories.

Recently, I found myself sharing this family story while visiting with Al and Edith Brafford, both of whom have a wealth of knowledge about Hope Mills history. Al Brafford said that the bell in the Cotton Mill No. 2, founded in 1888, was originally used to signal the mill workers when it was time to report to work. Years ago, it was also often used to sound local fire alarms. He told me the bell was located in a belfry four stories high. Then he smiled and said, "Lisa, I know where that old bell is if you would like to see it."

Evidently, when Cotton Mill No. 2 closed down, much of the equipment was purchased by the Elk Yarns mill on Legion Road. One day while visiting Elk Yarns, Mr. Brafford saw the old bell, recognized it as the bell taken out of the Cotton Mill No. 2 and asked Leonard Garner, the manager, if the company would be willing to give it or sell it back to the town because of its importance as a symbol of our history. The company agreed and actually donated the bell to the town.

The old bell now hangs securely in the belfry of the tower located adjacent to our town hall building. The date etched on the bell is *1891*. I have passed by the bell tower and that historical bell many, many times without ever giving it a second thought.

Now seeing that old bell will never be the same for me.

The Easter Chicks

A lot of things may have changed over the years, but one thing has remained the same—the excitement that is generated by children at an Easter egg hunt. When I was a kid, Tart's TV sponsored a giant community Easter egg hunt. Tart's was a television and electronics store located on Bragg Boulevard in Fayetteville.

I guess the idea was to get parents to the store with their kids to hunt for eggs, hoping they would return at a later time to hunt for new televisions. Hundreds of kids and their parents would converge upon an open field behind Tart's on the day of the event. Some kids would be armed with straw baskets and others with plastic buckets or plain paper bags. Thousands of candy eggs, wrapped in clear plastic wrappers, were "hidden" throughout the field in fairly obvious places. After someone gave the signal to begin, children would take off running in all different directions, searching the ground for eggs and filling their baskets with the ones they were lucky enough to discover.

But the very best part of the event took place when the Easter egg hunt was over. That is when Tart's TV would give away free live Easter chicks to the children. They weren't just plain old chicks either. They were dyed in bright Easter colors. Today, the very thought of that sounds barbaric and cruel to me, but back then for some reason I thought it was totally cool.

One Easter, we adopted three Easter chicks from the Tart's chick giveaway. My older brother picked out a blue one that he decided to name Bluey. My younger brother picked out a green chick that he called Greenie. And I, obviously being the most creative of the three children, had a pink chick named Butterball. The Easter chicks were placed in a cardboard box with a lamp over the top of the box to help keep them warm. We fed them dry grits and we gave them water in a jar lid.

As the chicks grew larger, they began to lose their colored pin feathers. All three chicks started to change from their bright Easter colors and emerge to become solid white chickens. That is when we were told that there was some kind of regulation that said we couldn't raise chickens in the city. The idea was discussed about taking the chicks to live at our grandmother's house.

Grandmother Carter, who lived in Massey Hill, had a fenced in area with a chicken coop in her backyard where she raised her chickens. So that is where the Easter chicks—Bluey, Greenie, and Butterball—were taken to live. On Sundays, we would go to visit my grandmother after church. My brothers and I would jump out of the car and run straight to her backyard to the chicken coop and check out the chickens. There were a lot of chickens and most all of them were solid white. "Which one is Greenie?" my brother would ask. My grandmother would point to a white chicken scratching at the ground in front of the door of the coop. Then I would ask, "Where's Butterball?" She would point to another chicken that would be scratching on the other side of the yard.

We would watch the chickens a while and play in the yard before being called inside the house for Sunday dinner, which usually featured Grandmother's specialty—homemade chicken and pastry.

I have to admit that I was well into my thirties before I finally put it all together and figured out the fate of old Bluey, Greenie, and Butterball, the Easter chicks. I am also really glad that I had a grandmother who understood that when it comes to certain things, they are better left untold.

Summer Memories

Well, it will soon be over. Summer, that is. I always judge that by when the stores begin to unpack back-to-school supplies and cartons are strewn throughout the aisles. Little white signs with red letters start going up around the store proclaiming "Back to School Sale." I used to hate that as a kid. Seeing the notebook paper, notebooks, composition books, and Number 2 pencils start coming out of boxes and going up on the shelves to replace the barbeque utensils, lounge chairs, inflatable beach balls, and box fans. I always hated to see summertime come to an end.

When my brothers and I were kids, summer was always the best time of year. Most of the daylight hours were spent outside playing with friends. In the morning, we would wake up early, no alarm clock necessary, eat breakfast, and head to the great outdoors. Every day was an adventure. We would wade in the creek and catch tadpoles.

We would spend a while building forts in the woods out of stuff we could find in the woods or around the neighborhood. Our favorite tree was our jungle gym and we would climb and swing from her limbs. During the heat of day, we would put on our bathing suits and jump over the sprinklers in the yard to cool off. We took breaks from time to time to drink water from the garden hose. It tasted funny, but it sure was good. Lunchtime, we drank lots of purple Kool-Aid and ate banana sandwiches.

In the afternoon, we would return to play hopscotch in the street. Fortunate enough to live on a cul-de-sac, there was very little traffic to worry the moms and dads. Of course, we didn't know we lived on a cul-de-sac. We always called it the "dead end circle." We didn't have chalk to draw our hopscotch blocks, so we improvised using soft chalky rocks we found down near the creek bank earlier in the day.

While we played, we listened for the music of the ice cream truck. When we heard it in the distance, we ran as fast as we could to get our quarters and made a beeline back to catch the truck before it got away. Waiting in line, we were forced to make the tough decision between the orange push-up and nutty buddy. We would eat our ice cream and finish up late afternoon with a game of "Mother May I," "Red Light, Green Light," or "Freeze Tag."

The initial glow of the streetlights signaled it was time to come home for dinner. We would wash up, eat dinner as a family and since there was no school, we would be allowed to return outdoors for a game or two of "Kick the Can." Sometimes we had as many as twenty neighborhood children playing together. Every now and then, some parents would join in, making it all the more fun!

If we got tired of "Kick the Can," we would substitute another game, like "Shadow Tag"—chasing each other's shadows around under the streetlights. My older brother sometimes used his imagination to create new games. One he called "Fox Chase Deer." Somehow, I always managed to end up as the fox. Another game was called "Snake in the Gutter." Yes, I always ended up as the snake. When I would finally figure out what was going on, he would quickly change to another game.

In the evening, we sat on the front porch reminiscing about the day's adventures and maybe even catching a firefly or two. Finally, it would be time to come in, take our baths, and get ready for bed. We would say our prayers, go to bed, sleep hard, and get up to start all over the next morning. Every day was about the same but every experience each day seemed brand new. These experiences turned into a collection of precious summer memories.

We didn't realize it at the time, but while we were collecting our summer memories, we were also learning a lot about life. We learned how to be patient, to wait in line, and to take turns. We learned how to play fair and cooperate in groups, how to win and lose, and how to give and take. We learned that if you aren't careful, you could be manipulated into becoming the fox or the snake all the time.

We learned how to appreciate and make use of things in our environment. Those summer experiences taught us how to be resourceful, organize, make decisions, and plan ahead. We learned how to figure out life. What was best, with the exception of the quarter for the ice cream, it cost next to nothing to stay entertained for an entire day, to exercise and to get plenty of fresh air. And maybe with the exception of the streetlight, there was little or no electricity involved.

Maybe it's me, but this summer I haven't noticed many kids outdoors. Maybe it's air-conditioning. Maybe it is the video games, technology, and television. Maybe it is the constant bombardment of depressing news about some of the terrible, horrible things that happen to children these days. Maybe it is a combination of it all. But it just doesn't seem right not to see kids playing outdoors during the summer.

My greatest wish is that every child be given the opportunity to experience the great outdoors, to learn through play with friends and family, and to develop their own personal collections of precious summer memories to carry with them through life. Yes, the stores are signaling us that summer will soon be over but it's not too late. We still have a little time. So if you get a chance, please take a kid outdoors to play!

Halloween

Halloween has always been one of my favorite holidays. As a kid, it was all about costumes, trick or treating, and the annual school carnival. Late Halloween afternoon, we would begin making our way up the street, armed with paper grocery bags used to load our candy, stopping at every door along the way.

On our street, the two most popular houses for treats were the Parks' and the Sherman's. Mrs. Parks always handed out homemade caramel popcorn balls. Everyone would try to get to her house before she ran out of them. Mr. Sherman, who lived across the street from the Parks, would dress up in a gorilla suit each Halloween. He would sit in his dimly lit foyer and wait for the doorbell to ring. Then he would open the door and jump out to scare us.

Of course, we knew it was him and we knew he was going to do it each year. But it would always make us jump and scream anyway.

Our Halloween trick or treating expedition would take us all the way to our final destination—the elementary school. That is where we spent the rest of the evening at the school-sponsored Halloween carnival.

One of the things I now enjoy around Halloween time is watching all the spooky movies that accompany the season. Two weeks before Halloween, the American Movie Classics channel airs it annual Monster Fest.

For us scary movie lovers, it is something we look forward to each year.

Monster Fest consists of thirteen days and nights of teeth-chattering, hair-raising classic horror movies. I have spent the past thirteen days watching such thrillers as Frankenstein Meets the Space Monster, The Fog, Earth vs. the Spider, Psycho, Poltergeist, and John Carpenter's movie Halloween with each of its five sequels.

I am not really sure where I developed such an affinity for horror shows. I suspect it must have been from growing up watching Alfred Hitchcock Presents and Sunrise Theatre.

Alfred Hitchcock Presents was a thirty-minute TV show hosted by the master of suspense himself, Alfred Hitchcock. His anthologies would not only frighten you, they kept you right on the edge of your seat in anticipation as you watched.

Sunrise Theatre aired each Saturday morning around daybreak. On the day, most school kids would probably choose to sleep in, I would be up with my eyes glued to the television set watching Sunrise Theatre.

Sunrise Theatre featured scary movies, many of which have now become classics. Most were filmed in black and white. Saturday morning you could watch the Creature from the Black Lagoon, a humanoid amphibious fish creature, as it terrorized an Amazon expedition, or *Mothra*, a giant monster moth, as it flew across the ocean to avenge the honor of a family dynasty.

Some Saturdays, there were movies about Godzilla and King Kong. Sometimes the movies were about confrontations between Godzilla and other monsters. But the movie that always scared me the most for some reason was House of Wax, starring Vincent Price.

Something about Vincent Price and that boiling vat of wax made my skin crawl.

During Sunrise Theatre, I would sit on the floor in front of the television with my brothers, eating cereal. My dad would sneak into the kitchen at some point, ease up from behind, and scare us.

Much like it was with Mr. Sherman in his gorilla suit, we always knew he was going to do it, but it still made us jump and scream anyway.

I guess for me, Saturday morning Sunrise Theatre has now officially been replaced by the AMC annual Monster Fest. I don't jump and scream anymore, but I still sit with my eyes glued to the television and have a really good time.

Hopefully, this Halloween night will feature some real spine-tinglers.

Family Historical Tour

I went on a group tour to learn more about my family history. Some of us rode together in a rented van, driven by my cousin Robert Love Carter. My father sat in the front passenger seat, serving as our tour guide. My two aunts followed close behind in a car. Altogether, there were thirteen members in our group with one common connection: We are all descendants of, or married to descendants of, Love and Mary Cashwell Carter from the Gray's Creek community.

Love and Mary Carter had six children: Jessie Pearl Carter, Sudie Carter Riddle, Calton Derb Carter, Mary "Mame" Carter Tyson, Jack Cashwell Carter, and Mabel Carter Council. All six children lived in the Gray's Creek area for a major part, if not all of their lives. Upon the death of their parents, the family farm was divided among these six children. Most all of the land still remains property of the descendants of Love and Mary Carter.

Our historical family tour actually began at Massey Hill School. My father, his brother, and his two sisters graduated from Massey Hill High School. A first cousin, Geraldine Tyson Davis, taught ninth grade there in 1939.

Melba Davis Whatley, from Austin, Texas, was one of the members of our touring group. She is the daughter of Geraldine Tyson Davis and the granddaughter of Mary "Mame" Carter Tyson. Her mother died when Melba was just twenty-two years of age. As an only child, Melba said she was eager to learn as much as she could about her family history and to hear all the stories.

Our next stop was at the homeplace of my grandparents, Calton Derb Carter and his wife Lela Horner Carter in Massey Hill. That is the home where my aunt Harriet Jean Carter was born and still resides. During this part of the tour, we learned that my grandfather Carter purchased the house in Massey Hill in 1929 for $1000. At that time, he was serving as a deputy sheriff in Cumberland County. My grandfather moved his family from Gray's Creek to Massey Hill because the Cumberland County commissioners had passed a regulation in 1929 requiring all deputies to have telephones. The county had agreed to pay for the phones. At that time, there wasn't a telephone, or electricity, within five miles of my grandfather's residence in Gray's Creek. The move was made in order to get closer to town to meet the new county telephone regulation.

At this stop, we heard familiar stories about my grandfather's infamous long legs and his big feet, good for chasing bootleggers through the surrounding woods and swamps in Cumberland County. My grandfather also served as police chief in Hope Mills in 1938–39.

Our next stop on the tour was the old Fisher Cemetery located next to Grandson's Restaurant on Chicken Foot Road. That is where we visited the gravesites of my great-great-grandparents, J. N. and Mary Ann Cashwell.

They were the parents of Mary Cashwell who later married Love Carter.

Next the tour bus circled through the parking lot of the new Gray's Creek High School. This school replaced the old Gray's Creek School, which was located on School Road. Then we visited the old Gray's Creek School, which now serves as a middle school.

Several members of our touring party, including Joe and Judy Carter Hardison, Robert Carter and Bunting "Bunti" Riddle Russ, graduated from the old Gray's Creek School. My father attended the school in grades 1 and 7.

At this site, Bunti Russ shared a story about a fire at the school. Her father, Durham Riddle, was meeting at the Ruritan Club next door when it occurred. He and several others ran into the burning building and helped to save important school papers and student records from being destroyed.

At this stop, we learned that my grandfather drove a bus for the Gray's Creek School before he married my grandmother.

Our next stop was Green Spring Baptist Church. It was there that we visited the gravesites of Love and Mary Carter and three of their children—Jessie Pearl Carter, Calton Derb Carter, and Mabel Carter Council.

We heard a story about Aunt Mabel and how she gained notoriety in the community when she shot the head off of a large snake. We also heard that Aunt Mabel, and her older sister Pearl, did not always see eye-to-eye on things.

Our tour continued on to the Durham and Lucy Riddle's homeplace. There we admired the beautiful yard filled with colorful camellias. Durham Riddle was the son of Augustus "Gus" and Sudie Carter Riddle. Driving a little further down the road, we arrived at Aunt Sudie's old homeplace. There we saw the large room, located in the back of the house, where Aunt Sudie would host the popular community quilting bees.

We traveled on to the Love Carter's homeplace on Yarborough Road. We learned that the original Love Carter house was a one-and-a-half-story log structure. Later, an addition to the home was built on the site. Water was drawn from an open well, fed by a natural spring. There was also a tobacco barn on the property.

We listened to stories about the garden, the pecan trees and the black walnut trees. We learned that some of the wood from the black walnut trees was purchased and shipped overseas to England. It was later discovered that the seller had marketed it as lumber from the mountains of North Carolina, believing that doing so would bring top price as high quality wood.

The Love Carter farm also had a tar kiln located on the property. Turpentine and other naval stores were made from the sap of the longleaf pines that grew abundantly on the farm. A marshy area called "Pocosin swamp" was known for its wild huckleberries, blueberries, and red bugs. Aunt Pearl's home was located very close to the Love Carter home. We learned that Aunt Mabel, who inherited the Love Carter's homeplace, later traded properties with my grandfather in order to get a little distance between her and her sister Pearl.

Our next stop took us to the Mary "Mame" Carter Tyson's homeplace. Along with Melba, another one of Aunt Mame's granddaughter's, Sarah Black, was on our tour. She and her husband Ed made a special trip from Florida to join our group. We learned that Aunt Mame's yard was used to manufacture syrup from sugar cane. A mule would walk in circles, hitched to the grinder that ground the cane stalks to remove the sugar. The sugar was then heated and made into syrup.

We traveled on to see the homeplace of Jack Cashwell Carter and his wife Myrtle. Jack Carter was a farmer, an avid rabbit and fox hunter and was well-known as the community barber, cutting hair for family and neighbors.

We passed the second home of Mabel Carter Council and her husband Len. We also visited the original homeplace of Calton Derb Carter that he later traded to his sister Mabel. That is the home where my father, his sister Jessie, and his brother Lentz were born.

Our tour ended at Bladen Union Church. There we visited the gravesites of Sudie Carter Riddle and her husband Augustus, Mary "Mame" Carter Tyson and her husband Walter, and Jack and Myrtle Carter's infant son who died at birth. Jack Cashwell Carter and his wife, Myrtle, are both buried in Lafayette Cemetery in Fayetteville.

It was at Bladen Union Church that I left the tour. But I understand the van traveled on from there to St. Paul's and made a few other stops along the way. I am really glad I went on this historical family tour.

I learned a lot, I took lots of pictures, and we videotaped all the stories to keep them in our family for generations to come. I think everyone should go on a group tour to learn more about their family history.

Part II

On Marriage

TILL DEATH DO US PART

Old Bedroom Slippers

Working in a job that often requires me to stand on my feet all day, I truly understand the meaning of the phrase "as comfortable as an old shoe." I own an old pair of bedroom slippers that have brought comfort to my feet for several years. They are now worn with age and are getting in such bad shape that I know it is time to replace them. I have kept putting it off, however, because I love those old bedroom slippers.

I returned from my last trip with cramped toes, aching feet, and a blister on my right heel. This was the result of wearing a pair of cute, but uncomfortable, shoes all day. When I arrived home, I got out of my car and hobbled into the house. I took off my shoes and headed straight to find my bedroom slippers. I can't begin to describe the relief I felt when I slipped those old, comfortable shoes onto my tired, aching feet.

My bedroom slippers were purchased in an airport store. I was waiting for my plane and went into the store just to look around. The bedroom shoes happened to be on sale. According to the salesperson, these particular slippers were designed using a special foam material developed by scientists for NASA. The foam was placed in the astronauts' seats to ensure them a more comfortable ride during space travel. Impressed, I decided to try on a pair.

I am not sure if it was because I had been on my feet all day or if the slippers were actually that unbelievably comfortable, but the minute I tried them on I was sold. It felt as though I was walking on two puffy clouds. The bottoms of the slippers conformed to the bottoms of my feet and the tops were made out of a stretchy material that cradled my toes without pressing against them. If it hadn't been for the fact that I was in the airport, I would have probably worn them home that day. Not only did I buy those bedroom slippers, I actually purchased another pair just like them for Mike. Unfortunately, they only came in one color, navy blue, making size the only difference between my slippers and my husband's. During the past two years, this has presented a small problem.

Often, both pairs of slippers are lying around on the bedroom floor and it is difficult to know which pair you are slipping on, especially if it is dark. You must check first by trying them on to make sure you have the correct pair. I have always made it a point to check. It is easy for me to know if I have slipped on his pair by mistake. They are too big and they are hard to keep on my feet. I have suspected all along, however, that my husband doesn't check. My suspicion has been that he just crams his feet into the first pair of slippers he finds on the floor and wears them. Since they are made of the stretchy foam material, he can get my shoes on his feet. His heels hang off the back, but for some reason that doesn't seem to bother him.

My suspicion came to light the other day when I realized that someone, with a much bigger foot than mine, must have been forcing their feet into my shoes for quite some time. A small hole wearing at the end of my right shoe had completely broken through, exposing my big toe. When I confronted him, Mike confessed he had occasionally been wearing my slippers. He told me that there was a small sharp object, like a nail or tack, starting to work its way up through the bottom of one of his own slippers, causing him discomfort when he walked. He had secretly resorted to wearing mine whenever they were available.

I have a birthday just around the corner. Knowing him like I do, I suspect he may be thinking of replacing my old bedroom slippers for some new ones for my birthday. So I decided to let him in on a little secret of my own. About three months ago, my travels found me once again in the same store where I had purchased our bedroom slippers. Anticipating that the day would eventually come when we would need to replace them, I purchased two more pairs of the identical slippers. I kept these hidden away in unopened boxes.

Now we both have a brand new pair of navy blue slippers. Hopefully, they will serve us as well as our original ones. And since old habits die hard, this time around there will be no mistaking which ones are mine – they are the pair with the pink pom-poms attached.

A Crappie Day

The first time Mike announced he wanted to take me crappie fishing on Hope Mills Lake, I thought to myself, Why would I want to catch crappie fish? Little did I know that crappie were not only a legitimate kind of fish, they also happen to provide southern sportsmen and women with one of the most fun fishing experiences possible on a freshwater pond or lake. Why?

I was told it was because if you do happen to get lucky enough to catch one, they don't go down without a good fight. I remember looking out at the lake that morning and wondering if there were really all that many crappie fish out there. After all, Hope Mills Lake, even in all her glory, was not the ocean. However, Mike assured me there were plenty of fish out there and they were just waiting to be caught.

So being a good sport, I decided I would give it a try.

There were several important decisions that had to be made. The first decision was to determine the necessary supplies for the fishing trip. I packed sodas, several sandwiches, crackers, chips and an extra large thermos of coffee. I figured that if we somehow became stranded on the lake, we would at least need enough grub to maintain us a day or two.

The next decision concerned appropriate fishing attire. I was told I should wear comfortable clothing and rubber-soled shoes. I was also informed that sunglasses and a hat with a brim were both required. These items would help cut down the amount of glare from the water and keep the sun out of my eyes so I could see all the fish. Sunglasses weren't a problem but I had to find a hat.

After searching through closets, I discovered an old baseball cap with the letter T on it like one I had observed Bill Dance wearing on one of his Saturday morning fishing shows. I figured if it were good enough for Bill, it would be good enough for me. I packed it in with the rest of my stuff.

The final decision was securing the right bait, which according to Mike, was probably the most important decision of all. So off we went to Rita's Bait Shop. I had never been in Rita's Bait Shop so of course I had to look around a little before we shopped for bait. I was amazed to find all kinds of interesting things in the store, ranging from fishing gear to groceries. There was also a large tank filled with shiny little minnows.

Mike announced that they would make great crappie bait.

I peered through the glass at the tiny little fish swimming innocently around in the tank completely unaware they were about to become crappie food. I really felt sorry for them but was told we needed at least a couple of dozen. I tried to pick out the bigger ones that looked like they had a fighting chance to get away.

As we left with our minnows, I began giving them names. Mike informed me that it wasn't such a good idea, so I just stopped looking in the bucket.

Armed with fishing poles and tackle, we put everything we had accumulated in the boat and went out on the lake. Mike said we had to search for what he called a "good spot." Funny, when you are on the water, all the spots seem to look the same. We rode around a little while and he finally brought the boat to a stop and threw out the anchor.

He baited the hooks, which I refused to do for obvious reasons, and threw out the two lines in the water.

We both sat quietly and I stared at the orange bobber thing on my line floating aimlessly around in the water. I was mesmerized by the sound of the water rippling beneath the boat. After a while, my husband looked over at me and asked, "What are you thinking about?" I replied, "The orange bobber thing floating around in the water."

"Exactly!" he said. "Isn't it great?"

Believe it or not, we did catch a lot of crappie fish that day. I also learned a lot of things about fishing.

Interestingly enough, the most important thing I learned is that fishing isn't really about catching fish.

It is about experiencing nature, getting your mind off the worries of life, just relaxing and listening to the sound of the water rippling beneath a boat.

It is about being in tune with oneself and being totally at peace.

I understand now why so many people like to fish, and I am really looking forward to the day I can once again go crappie fishing on Hope Mills Lake with Mike. You know, I guess it's not so bad to have a crappie day after all!

The Lawn Mower

When I decided to try cutting the grass on a riding mower, I just assumed all of my good driving skills would easily transfer and that mastering the mower would be a piece of cake. Unfortunately, it did not work out that way.

It all started the morning I looked outside at the front lawn and saw the field of bright yellow dandelions overtaking the yard. They were almost knee-high and seemed to have sprung up overnight. I knew something had to be done and that it couldn't wait so I headed to the garage. There in the far corner of the garage sat my husband Mike's prized possession—his bright green and yellow John Deere riding lawn mower. I went over to check it out. For some reason, this piece of equipment had always been off limits to me. Mike is the one who mows the grass. He treats his John Deere mower more like a baby than a machine.

But how difficult could operating it be? The key was in the ignition and it looked as if the mower were sitting there ready to help solve my dandelion problem. I thought all I had to do was crank her up, step on the gas, and drive out of the garage and onto the lawn. Then I would simply ride back and forth in a diagonal pattern in order to make those pretty stripes in the yard that I usually see when Mike cuts the grass.

I opened the garage door and climbed up on the seat of the mower. I turned the key as if I were attempting to crank my car. Nothing happened. I tried again and still nothing happened. That is when I realized that perhaps this was going to be a little more complex than I first anticipated.

As much as I hated to do it, I made the dreaded phone call to my husband to tell him my intentions and ask for some instructions. At first, he told me that I didn't need to cut the lawn because he was planning to do it in the next couple of days. However, when he heard me talk about knee-high dandelions and what the neighbors must be thinking, he eventually conceded and told me I could try but I needed to be very careful.

My first instructions were about how to crank the mower. He described a six-step process to accomplish the task. It took a few minutes and my hearing the instructions several times but I finally was successful in getting the lawn mower to crank. Delighted, I stepped on the gas pedal and drove out of the garage for a test drive on the lawn. I decided to begin near the front porch up close to the house. I drove over the sidewalk near the porch and began to cut the grass. Things seemed to be going very well but after my second pass I started to notice grey fuzzy stuff on the lawn. Curious, I looked over my shoulder as I continued to mow. There was a lot of grey fuzzy stuff all over the ground behind me. That's strange, I thought to myself.

Then suddenly the mower came to an unexpected stop. I quickly tried the six-step cranking process; however, the mower would not crank. I got off the mower and went over to get a closer look at the grey fuzzy stuff that now covered my yard. That is when I realized that I was looking at the remains of what used to be our welcome mat. Evidently, when I drove over the sidewalk I had completely annihilated the mat. A lot of the mat was scattered in the yard, but a lot of it was still gnarled tightly around the blades of the lawn mower. My heart skipped a beat.

What would Mike say?

I reached underneath the mower and tried to pull what was left of the mat loose but it wouldn't budge. I rotated the blades and after some pulling and tugging, I finally managed to unwrap the welcome mat from around the blades of the lawn mower. I jumped back on the John Deere, followed my six-step cranking instructions, and went on to mow the rest of the lawn. When I finished I stepped back to admire my work. To my horror, there were no pretty stripes in the lawn. There was a patchwork of bald spots crisscrossing all over my front yard. Turns out one side of the lawn mower blade had dropped lower than the other side during the tug-of-war with the welcome mat.

Who knows? Maybe I inherited a propensity for problems on a riding lawn mower. The first time my mother attempted to mow the lawn using one, she ended up taking out an entire bed of azaleas. The only thing that stopped her and the mower from plowing through the neighbor's patio was a pine tree. I guess I can always buy another welcome mat. Fortunately, my grass will eventually grow back.

Unfortunately, it will also have to be mowed.

Fussy in the House

The other evening, we ordered a pizza for home delivery. It was dark outside, so I turned on the front porch light. Thirty minutes later, a car pulled into the drive and I saw a young lady driver emerge with our pizza. I opened the door and turned to retrieve the money for payment I had placed on the table near the door. I gave the young lady the money and she removed the cardboard box from its warming sleeve.

"You got birds?" she asked, as she handed me the pizza. I looked at her a little puzzled. We have a parrot but her cage is in a room out of sight of the front door. Mildred wasn't talking or squawking at the time, so how would this delivery lady know about her? "We have a parrot," I replied with a little hesitation. "Why do you ask?"

"Oh, I thought I saw a little bird flying around in your house," she said, looking past me. I assured her Mildred was secure in her cage and there were no birds flying around inside our house. "Well then, I must be seeing things," she said, slowly shaking her head as she returned to her car.

I took the pizza into the kitchen, amused by her strange comment. That is when the little brown bird fluttered past me, across the kitchen, and into the living room. For a moment I stood in total disbelief, suddenly realizing the pizza delivery lady had not been seeing things at all.

"We got birds!" I yelled to Mike. "I thought we were getting pizza," he said, coming into the kitchen. I pointed to the tiny brown bird now sitting under a chair in our living room. I told him about the comment from the pizza delivery lady and how she left thinking she was seeing imaginary birds flying around in our house.

"It's Fussy!" Mike said.

Fussy is the name of the little Carolina wren that roosts on an eave of our front porch at night. The porch light must have scared him when I turned it on for the pizza delivery. He had somehow flown undetected into the house when the door opened. We opened the front door again in hopes Fussy would fly back outside. Instead, he flew from the living room, down the hallway, and into our bedroom. There we found him perched on top of a window curtain. I made one failed attempt to capture him with a pillow case but he was just too fast. Finally, he flew back down the hallway and landed on the light fixture in the entry hall.

We stood quietly nearby, again hoping he would discover the front door still standing open for him. After a few moments, Fussy took off out the door to the safety of a nearby boxwood bush. My husband went to the kitchen for pizza and I went for the phone.

"Who are you calling?" he asked, munching on a slice of pizza.

I told him I was calling the pizza place so they could tell the delivery lady that she wasn't seeing things and that we really did have a bird flying around inside our house. "I don't want her to think she is crazy," I said.

"No, they will just think you are crazy," he said. Perhaps, but I say all's well that ends well.

Much To-Do About Thai Food

A few weeks ago, I ordered pizza in an airport restaurant. They had several unique varieties from which to choose.

I decided to order one that was made with Thai peanut sauce and traditional Thai vegetables, just to try something a little different from the usual pepperoni and mushroom we order at home.

I had never eaten Thai food before and I must say it was really good.

The following week, I was traveling again and came across a Thai restaurant. I decided to eat my dinner there. I explained to the waitress that I had only eaten Thai food once, but it was in the form of pizza, so I wasn't sure that counted. I described the pizza I had at the airport and told her I really liked the peanut sauce. She said I should consider ordering the Chicken Pad Thai. She said it could be made with a peanut sauce like I had on my pizza.

So that's what I ordered and just like the Thai pizza, it was really good.

When I returned home from my trip, I decided I would try making a Thai dish. I looked up the recipe for Chicken Pad Thai on the internet, wrote it down, and went to the store to purchase the necessary ingredients.

I intentionally left the Thai rice noodles on the counter.

My husband Mike is a meat and potato person and his favorite flavor of ice cream is vanilla. I thought leaving the package of rice noodles on the counter would mentally prepare him for the fact that I was going to venture out and cook something different from his usual desired cuisine.

I cooked the Chicken Pad Thai according to the internet recipe, changing one or two things so it would look more like the

Pad Thai I had in the restaurant. When dinner was served, the following conversation ensued.

Mike: What is that?

Lisa: It's called Chicken Pad Thai.

Mike: Why did you put an egg on top of it?

Lisa: Because that is how they served it in the Thai restaurant in California.

Mike: Are those crushed peanuts on top of that egg?

Lisa: Yes.

Mike: Don't tell me. Let me guess. That's how they did it in the restaurant.

Lisa: Yep.

Mike: You know, I don't really like Thai food.

Lisa: Have you ever tried Thai food?

Mike: No, because I don't like it.

Lisa: Then don't eat it.

Mike: But I'm hungry.

Lisa: Then eat it. I'm just trying to learn how to cook Thai food.

Mike: I don't think I would like it even if the person cooking it knew what they were doing.

Lisa: (Silence)

Mike: I was kind of hoping we were having meat and some vegetables.

Lisa: There's chicken in there.

Mike: Well, I really wanted some vegetables. (Lifting the egg and looking beneath it)

Lisa: There are vegetables in there.

Mike: (Lifting the egg again and looking again) Where?

Lisa: There's bean sprouts and green onions mixed in it.

Mike: Those aren't real vegetables.

Lisa: Oh yes, they are!

Mike: All right, I'll try it but only because I'm starving to death.

Although Mike only picked out the chicken, the meal was not a total lost cause. At least he now knows why he doesn't like Thai food and I know to stick to ordering real Thai dishes in my travels.

Christmas Tree Drama

Each year during the first week of December, a holiday drama occurs in our living room. Unfortunately, the general public is not invited. However, if I did sell tickets, I think I could make a lot of money.

This drama takes place the night Mike and I put up our artificial Christmas tree. When it comes to this seasonal ritual, we have established our routines and responsibilities that are unspoken but understood.

Basically, my job is to pick out the spot in the living room where I want to place the tree. Mike's job is to go upstairs, drag down the tree and all the boxes of decorations from where they are stored throughout the year, set up the tree in the living room, and place the boxes of decorations and a ladder next to the tree.

He also makes sure all the lights on the tree are working properly. From there, I take over. I fluff out all the squashed branches and meticulously place the ornaments and decorations on the tree. Mike's last job is to return for the final inspection and brag about what a good job I have done decorating the tree.

Now you would think that putting up an artificial Christmas tree would be a relatively simple task, requiring very little thought or effort. Not so in our home.

Case in point, last week I decided it was time to put up the tree. Things began in much the usual way. I picked out a good spot in the living room and Mike went upstairs after the tree, decorations, and ladder. He brought the ladder and boxes of decorations into the living room and placed the tree upright in its stand.

Everything seemed to be going fairly smoothly until he got down on the floor and squeezed up under the bottom branches of the tree to tighten the screws in the stand.

"Is this the right stand?" he asked after a few minutes.

"Yes," I replied.

"Are you sure?"

I assured him it was.

He finally emerged from under the limbs and asked if I thought the tree looked straight. I told him it was leaning over to the right.

He crawled back under the tree and fiddled around some more with the screws, asking me to hold the tree up straight in the stand.

"Is it straight now?"

"I'm not sure." Frankly, it is hard to hold the tree and check to see if it is straight at the same time. After a few minutes, he reappeared from under the tree. This time, the tree was leaning over to the left and tilted backward toward the window.

He tried adjusting the screws and positioning the tree several more times, but each time it remained crooked, just in different directions. Frustrated, he took a magazine and stuffed it underneath one leg of the tree stand.

"That should take care of it!" he said.

Personally, I still thought the tree was leaning a little toward the left, however at this point, I wasn't about to say anything.

Next, he asked me if the tree seemed well-balanced in the stand. One year, we had a fully decorated tree fall over unexpectedly during Christmas, so this was a concern. I shook the metal trunk and it wiggled around a little. Mike went in the garage and returned with two large ten-pound weights, placing them in the bottom of the stand on either side to balance the tree.

"Now it is not going anywhere," he proudly exclaimed.

I didn't say a word, but he did the exact same thing last year and it looked absolutely ridiculous. The weights created these giant lumps under the tree skirt. I had to use Christmas presents to cover them up so no one would see them.

Cringing, I knew the worst part of the evening was yet to come. He had to test the tree lights. You see, Mike doesn't have much patience with the tree lights. One time, when he was trying to fix them, they became so entangled on the tree with so many of them failing to work that he actually unplugged the tree, took a pair of scissors out of the drawer, and cut them all off the tree.

Holding my breath, I watched nervously to see what would happen when he plugged the lights in for the test. Of course, not all the lights came on. He went all around the tree checking, unplugging and replugging the strings of lights. This caused the majority of them to light up. He grabbed the rest of the stringers and shook them violently until the remainder of the lights finally flickered on. "Loose bulbs," he mumbled.

Relieved, I took over from there, fluffed the branches, and decorated the tree.

Our tree is now up in the living room, ready to go for another holiday season. The lumps and bumps are handily camouflaged with colorful Christmas presents.

Mike did brag about how nice it looks even though in my opinion, it is still tilted a little over to the left.

Is It a Bear?

Last year, I gave Mike a "trail camera" as a birthday gift. A trail camera is often used by hunters to take pictures of wildlife in the woods. The camera, designed to be strapped to a tree, has an infrared light and a motion detector. When an object moves in front of it, the motion detector is triggered and the camera automatically snaps a picture. Instead of walking through the woods disturbing wildlife, the hunter can scout out potential prey by viewing pictures on a computer.

A week ago, Mike decided to set up his trail camera at the edge of the woods in one of his favorite hunting locations near Hope Mills. He pointed the camera toward a pile of deer corn in a field. He programmed the camera to take one picture every minute when its motion sensor was triggered.

He left the camera in the woods for a couple of days and then he returned to check the results. When he arrived home that evening, he had one of the pictures the camera had captured in his hand.

"Look at this," he said. "The camera took a picture of a black bear!"

Apparently, he was so excited he had taken the picture and had it enlarged to show everyone. He told me that he had never seen a bear in the woods as long as he had been hunting.

"Can you believe it?" he marveled, handing the picture over to me.

I looked at the dark shadowy figure in the bottom right hand corner of the picture. You couldn't see the entire animal or make out all of its features but you could tell it was an animal.

To me, it looked like a big black pig even though it was a little tall, perhaps a large wild hog that had escaped from a nearby farm.

"How do you know this isn't a large black pig?"

"It's a bear," Mike said. "Can't you see the size of the head on that thing?"

I looked at the picture again, this time trying to see a bear.

"It also looks like it could be a very large black Labrador Retriever sniffing at some corn," I said, still a bit skeptical. I pointed out what resembled the outline of the tip of the ear of a dog hanging down in front of the head of the animal.

"It's a bear," he said, adding that Labrador Retrievers do not have feet the size of tennis shoes. He told me that what I was calling the ear of a dog was actually the curve of the head of a bear.

At that point I stopped speculating and ended the discussion.

I smiled and told Mike I was glad he was enjoying his birthday present.

Bath Towels

I know that people shouldn't air their dirty laundry in public, but recently I just couldn't resist as the topic of conversation at a dinner gathering turned to bath towels. I shared a little about the ongoing towel debate in our home. I was actually rather surprised to hear that others had their own stories to tell. I guess when it comes to something as simple as an ordinary bath towel, everyone still has an opinion.

The towel controversy in our home centers around the number of times a towel should be used before it is placed in the laundry hamper. I grew up in a home where we were expected to use the same bath towel several times before trading it in for a new one. After a shower or bath, you were to hang up your towel in the bathroom, let it dry, and use it again the next day. I still subscribe to that basic philosophy when it comes to the use of towels.

Now certainly, there are a few exceptions to this towel rule. For example, if a towel somehow gets really soiled during its use, it should definitely go straight into the hamper or down the laundry shoot and not be used again until it is washed. But as a general rule, there is absolutely nothing wrong in using the same towel a few days in a row. Besides, it saves time, money and energy, and also conserves water because it cuts down on the amount of washing and drying that has to be done throughout the week.

For the longest time, I believed that using the same towel for multiple days was just standard practice for most people. Then I got married and discovered that is not necessarily the case. Mike believes that one must use a fresh, clean towel after each shower, no matter how many showers one takes per day. According to him, it is the only sanitary thing to do. He refers to his once-used towel as being dirty and he places it in the laundry to be washed immediately after its use. Each time he showers, he opens up the linen closet and retrieves a new, clean towel.

To make matters worse, when I hang my own towel in the bathroom as a model, he takes it down and uses it on the floor as his bath mat. Of course, this causes me to have to resort to securing another clean towel for my next shower. I refuse to use a towel that has been stomped all over the floor.

I have tried to convince Mike that there is nothing wrong with hanging up a towel, letting it dry, and using it for a second or even a third time. I have done it all my life and have never developed any kind of terrible towel disease as a result. So far, I haven't been able to persuade him.

From my estimates, we average around fourteen towels per week in the laundry just between the two of us. Some weeks it can be even more, as Mike sometimes will use two clean towels in one day. I actually have seen him get up in the morning and take a shower in order to go outside to mow the lawn. Afterwards, he needs another shower and, of course, another fresh towel. Seems to me that neither the first shower nor the first towel were really necessary.

Needless to say, towels pile up around our house week after week.

And they all have to be washed and dried.

Trying to keep up with the demand for clean towels in our home has resulted in the accumulation of a large variety of bath towels in the linen closet. We have a few really nice, thick fluffy towels that I like to use, even though they are bulky in the washer and take longer to dry. There are also some thin, worn towels that Mike likes to use the best. His very favorite ones are so frayed and threadbare, you can actually hold them up to light and see through them. All of these towels come in an assortment of colors, which presents another problem come laundry time because they can't be washed together in the same load.

As our worn-out towels are eventually replaced, I have decided it best to purchase only one type of towel in the future—extremely thin and completely white.

They will cost less, they will alleviate the laundry sorting problem, more of them will fit into the washer at once, and they will dry in less time. This may not solve the entire towel problem in our home, but at least in the future it may help to keep our dirty laundry just a little bit cleaner.

Christmas Lights

This year, I thought it would be a nice idea to add some outdoor Christmas lights for the holidays. I went to the store and purchased ten sets of eighteen-foot "rope lights" thinking that would be enough to take care of the area I wanted to decorate. The lights are called "rope lights" because they look like long plastic ropes with small lights inside of them. I decided to buy red, white, and blue lights for the project.

When I arrived back home from the store, Mike met me in the garage with a hammer and a pack of tiny nails. "Let's get this over with," he said.

Now experience has taught me that whenever my husband begins any project with the words "Let's get this over with," it is never a good sign. I also know that dealing with Christmas lights is not his favorite chore. However, I sloughed off the words honestly thinking that putting up a few Christmas lights would not be that big of a deal.

My job was to unpacked the lights and straighten them out. Also, I was in charge of the plastic clips designed to hold the lighted ropes in place and the package of nails. The procedure was to hand one plastic clip and two small nails to Mike.

He, in turn, would tack the clip in place along the outside of a wooden rail.

Thank goodness, there were extra clips in the package. After breaking the first two plastic clips with the hammer, my husband said the wooden rail was old and the plastic clips were cheap. He said the clips would probably break whenever they froze. I am not sure about that but I know quite a few of the tiny clips broke as he attempted to nail them in place. Some others broke when he tried to secure the lighted rope into the plastic clips.

I could tell he was getting frustrated but he didn't stop. He actually began singing a little song with the words "Oh, how I love Christmas" and continued to nail the fragile clips into place on the rail. I had never heard that song before and I think he was making it up.

After he finished securing half of the new rope lights in place on the outside of the railings, I stood back to take a look at them. Then I asked Mike if he thought they would show up better if they were placed up on top of the rail instead of on the outside of the rail. He looked at me, mumbled something under his breath, and then told me he thought the lights looked just fine right where they were placed.

I knew he was going to say that, so I told him I would make a deal with him.

If he would put the clips on top of the railings and move the lights for me, I would remove the old clips—the ones he had already hammered into place—as soon as he left to go deer hunting that afternoon. I figured that if I mentioned deer hunting, it would ease the tension a little.

I looked at the approximately ninety feet of lights he had already secured in place and then looked over to see his reaction to my proposal to move the lights. Bringing deer hunting into the negotiations must have worked because he smiled and slowly nodded his head in agreement. Actually, he was surprisingly gracious about it.

He even started to sing his little "Oh, how I love Christmas" song again as he started the job over.

We finally got half of the new rope lights secured to the top of the rails and decided to leave putting up the other half until the following day. That way my husband could go deer hunting and I could work to remove the clips off the side of the rails as we had agreed. Later that evening, I went outside to turn on the section of lights we had completed to see how they looked. I have to say that when I saw them lit up, I was disappointed. The colors just didn't look the way I had envisioned them.

When Mike returned from deer hunting that evening, he asked me what I thought about the lights. "I think the red lights look great, the white ones look okay, and the blue ones don't even show up," I said.

After seeing the lights and my disappointment, he agreed it would look better if all the lights were red. "We could save the white and blue ones for the Fourth of July," he said.

So the following day, I went back to the store to get more boxes of red rope lights. When I returned home, we worked together most of the afternoon to get them up. This time, things went along pretty smoothly, barring one minor splinter operation that I had to perform on my husband's trigger finger. During the operation, he again sang his little "Oh, How I Love Christmas" song. This time with his teeth clenched and without moving his lips.

We also discovered the fact that we were short one strand of lights and that one set we had already clipped into place didn't work. So with only two strands left to finish up the job, I went back to the store the following day to purchase two more strands of red lights. After thoroughly searching the shelves, I discovered the store had sold out all the red rope lights. It was at that moment that I caught myself singing my husband's "Oh, how I love Christmas" song in the store. I decided two packages of green rope lights would have to finish the job.

It took us three days but our red and green rope lights are up now and we are ready for the holidays. Mike did manage to bag an eight point buck in the process, and I learned a new song called "Oh, How I Love Christmas!"

Drama-Free Holiday Decorating

About this same time each year, I write something about the drama that inevitably goes on at our house while we are decorating for the Christmas holidays.

For example, one year it was the tree that once in place and fully decorated, distinctly tilted to the left despite my husband Mike's noble attempts to straighten it using old magazines placed beneath the stand. Another year, it was the tangled tiny white lights that were left on the artificial tree which had to be removed because so many bulbs had burned out. After wrestling with the string for an hour or so, Mike finally "fixed" the problem with a pair of scissors and some yanking.

Then there was the flagpole tree.

This holiday, decoration consists of strings of lights which attach to a flagpole in the yard to form a Christmas tree. Putting it up is always quite an ordeal. My husband recruited his brother Robbie to help him one year and the two put up the flagpole tree while I was out Christmas shopping.

The only problem was that they put it up on the wrong flagpole. They claimed I said, "Put it in the back." I claim I said, "Put it back where it was." Anyway, after some discussion, they were kind enough to move it to the other flagpole in the front yard where I wanted it.

I am happy to report that this year there has only been some minor drama that has occurred with our holiday decorating. It once again concerned the Christmas tree. While putting up the tree, we discovered an important part was missing. The missing part was a small piece of plastic that secures the top portion of the tree in its place. Without it, the top of the tree falls off.

First we checked for it by following our footsteps from the living room back to where the tree was stored to see if had dropped off during transport.

We couldn't find it.

Next, we searched through the mountain of nearby boxes to see if perhaps it had fallen into one of them.

The search turned up nothing.

Finally, Mike decided to attempt to fix it with one of his standard fixes for most problems—duct tape. It worked! The top of the tree is in place, the tree is fully decorated and all is well as we prepare for the holidays.

Only one word of warning, don't touch the Christmas tree. There is no guarantee how long the tape will stick.

Fly Swatting

Summer has not officially arrived, but it's hot. Along with the heat, there seems to be a lot of flies. I began noticing several flies buzzing about the house a few weeks ago.

At first I thought it was just me thinking it unusual for this time of year.

Then I heard Mike complaining about them. Mike hates flies.

If a fly gets in our house, it is doomed.

Mike is a master at exterminating a fly and won't rest until he has taken care of it.

The plastic swatter he uses as a weapon of choice is located on top of the refrigerator.

The handle is always strategically positioned to be within his easy reach. "Got it!" is his favorite phrase after he takes one out.

As for me, I never really got into killing flies.

If one got in the house, I would usually open the door and try to direct it to freedom. Lately, however, it seems that for each fly I escort out the door, three or four come in the door to take its place.

That is why recently I decided I would try my hand at fly swatting. Actually, I have gotten quite good at it.

I have discovered that becoming an accomplished fly exterminator requires three distinct skills—observation, patience, and determination. First, you have to watch the fly and try to follow its path with your eyes.

Then after it lands, you have to move slowly toward it.

You must oh so slowly and carefully raise the swatter without bringing attention to it.

Then you use your wrist to take a quick snap at the insect.

After some practice I decided to show off my new skill. "Watch this," I said to Mike, while backhanding a fly on the refrigerator with the plastic swatter. My husband appeared quite impressed and even commented on my technique. He said that particular fly must have gone through the kitchen wall and that I would probably find what was left of it in the laundry room. Of course, I was quite pleased with myself.

My new goal is to learn how to take two flies out in one swat.

I am confident that it won't be long before I accomplish it, with all the practice I am getting.

Refinished Floors

Having a hardwood floor refinished in your home is a long, drawn out, and messy process. It requires moving furniture and sanding the wood creates dust. The dust is like a fine mist and it has a way of traveling throughout your house.

Then there is the polyurethane.

The fumes from the polyurethane coating fill the air and it smells to high heaven. Usually, there are multiple coats that must be applied and each coat requires time to dry. You can't walk on the floor during this period.

So you can understand why I went with scratched up hardwood floors in our foyer until I could stand it no longer. When I could finally see the bare wood showing beneath the old finish, I decided enough was enough. After finding someone I felt confident could do the job, we cleared the foyer and dining room of all furniture in preparation.

The sanding wasn't so bad. The fellow doing the job used what is called dustless system which did minimize the dust. I also shut down the air-conditioning and covered up as much as I could. After the floors were sanded, it became more complicated. First I had to pick out the color of the finish. After much debate, I narrowed it down to three stains—cherry, English walnut, and early American.

I asked the floor guy to put samples on the floor for me to look at overnight. I finally made up my mind that I wanted the early American. The worker put the early American stain on two steps.

I made up my mind again.

I wanted the cherry stain.

He patiently obliged and the two steps were re-sanded, and the rest of the stain was applied to the floor.

Then, however, came the hardest part of all. The first coat of polyurethane had to be applied and allowed to dry for twenty-four hours. That meant no walking on it. The problem presented was that in order to get to a bathroom and to the bedroom, we had to walk through the foyer.

Now I wasn't too worried about that myself. You see, as luck would have it, I was leaving to go on a trip for three days.

I would be away during the polyurethane time.

Mike, on the other hand, would be at home. I really wasn't worried about him because being the avid hunter, who can survive for days out in the woods, I knew he would find a way to make due.

As I was packing to leave, he told me he had figured it all out. He would lean a ladder in the living room up to the second floor landing. Then he would climb up and down this ladder to the second floor to get to a bathroom and to go to bed in the evening.

"You will kill yourself," I told him.

"No, I won't," he said.

"What about Mousie?" I asked. Mousie, our little dog, sleeps upstairs with us.

"I will take Mousie with me." Sure enough, he had already placed Mousie's little pink carrier tied to a rope to raise and lower her.

Not only did Mike manage to make this work, he even climbed down in the middle of the night for a midnight snack, taking the snack back up the ladder with him in a paper sack. I should have known that a man who can climb a twenty-foot ladder up a tree and maneuver into a deer stand seat with a shotgun in tow would somehow turn this problem into memorable indoor sports adventure.

The Missing Eagle

Ladies and gentlemen, the story you are about to read is true. The names have been changed to protect the innocent. These events took place right here in Hope Mills. It is officially on record as case number 2012-02240—the case of the missing concrete eagle.

John Doe says he passed by the brick column situated at the end of his driveway several times early Monday morning while on his riding lawn mower cutting the grass. Everything seemed to be in order, John says, but he did notice a strange dark-colored stain on top of the brick column.

He says he wondered what had caused the stain since he had never noticed it there before.

It wasn't long after when Sam Doe, John's brother who was assisting with the yard work, inquired about the disappearance of a concrete eagle statue that had been on top of that same brick column.

It is at that moment that John says he realized that the eagle statue was, in fact, missing. The mysterious stain on top of the column must have been caused by dirt and debris that had accumulated beneath the statue over the years, he deducted.

John immediately looked at the three other brick columns at the end of the driveway—the other columns he had obviously mowed past several times that morning as well. Each of the three other columns had a concrete eagle statue still perched in its proper place.

John hurriedly sent a text message to his wife, Jane Doe, which read, "One of eagles at the end drive stolen." Jane's text back to John was, "No way."

After all, the eagle statue had been there for over seven years. Since it was made of concrete, it was extremely heavy. Who in the world could have taken it? Why would someone take the eagle and leave the three others?

If it were October, one might think it to be a kid's Halloween prank, but it was only early July.

No, the concrete eagle had not been bolted down on the brick column. That was the first question Jane was asked by the police investigator and a few curious amateur sleuths who have since heard the story.

Jane says the concrete bird was simply placed on top of the brick column without any thought that an eagle thief might one day be lurking around the neighborhood. Besides, Jane declares that the concrete statue was so heavy she couldn't lift it herself. She suspects someone had to really struggle in order to walk off with it.

Now the tiny angel that sits on Jane's right shoulder is whispering in her ear that someone must have really wanted that concrete eagle very badly but hopefully, through guilt, whoever took it will have second thoughts about their foul deed and return it back to its rightful place.

However, the tiny devil that sits on Jane's left shoulder is whispering in her ear that she might as well face the fact that she won't ever see her concrete eagle again but hopefully, through karma, whoever took the heavy statue is now sporting a painful hernia.

Jane did have the three remaining eagles at the end of the driveway transported to a safer location which will not be disclosed due to the possibility that the eagle thief could be reading this. An official report concerning this incident has been properly filed with the Hope Mills Police Department. According to Jane and John Doe's paperwork, the case status is listed as "Closed/Leads Exhausted." From all accounts, that is probably accurate since there were no leads to follow up on.

Apparently, no one saw anything and it is pretty safe to say, the other eagles aren't talking.

On Turning Fifty

There are milestones in our lives that mark significant events. I just experienced one of those major milestones. I turned fifty. Yes, me. I am now officially a half-century old. Although I tried hard not to show it, I had a little trouble accepting this particular milestone.

Sure, I believe that age is only a state of mind and that you are only as old as you feel. Yes, I know many older people who I think are really young because of their attitude and the way they approach life. But even so, I still had a problem with the idea of turning fifty years old.

I remember back in the sixties thinking anyone who was thirty was over-the-hill. Then when I actually turned thirty, I found out that it wasn't all that bad. In fact, I had a great time in my thirties. I guess I had learned a lot about life by then and what I had learned actually helped me to thoroughly enjoy the decade. Forty, of course, was also dreaded, but not so terribly much because thirty had turned out pretty good.

So you would think that I would have also had a decent attitude about entering my fifties, but I didn't. This birthday was the one I dreaded the very most. Turning fifty, after all, is the equivalent of living half a century and something about that just sounded really old to me! I wasn't sure how to handle my approaching birthday. I actually wanted to figure out a way to keep it from coming—to try to stay forty-nine forever. I decided to use an age-old tactic, ignore the problem until it goes away.

For weeks, I tried not to think about my upcoming birthday. But then things like AARP invitations and brochures begin to arrive in the mail. Still determined to remain forty-nine, I would just rip them up into tiny pieces and bury them deep in the trash.

I would use the remote to quickly switch channels when television celebrities would attempt to remind me I would soon be eligible for insurance and burial benefits for those fifty years of age and older. Then one by one, birthday cards, many of them explicit about the decade I was entering, began to appear in my mailbox.

Since they were from beloved friends and relatives, I did read them and displayed them neatly throughout the house. However, seeing them only served as another reminder of the dreaded day I was trying so desperately to forget. Finally, the clincher came just a few days before my actual birthday. My own father handed me a fifty-cent piece, a reminder, he said, just in case I forgot I was getting ready to turn fifty years old. In the midst of all these distractions, however, I continued to focus like a laser onto hanging on at forty-nine and not letting go.

Finally, the day before my birthday arrived. My work causes me to travel and I happened to be in California, sitting at the airport waiting on my plane. As nightfall approached, I was getting more desperate by the hour. Then a thought suddenly occurred. If I were at home in Hope Mills, North Carolina, I would turn fifty at midnight.

Being on Pacific Coast time gave me a three-hour reprieve. Midnight in Hope Mills is only 9:00 p.m. California! This thought triggered another thought and I was actually considering checking with the gate agent about the time difference in Hawaii, when I suddenly decided to just give up—to call it quits. I knew my efforts to stop my birthday from coming were all in vain. Defeated, I knew how the Grinch must have felt when he tried to stop Christmas from coming and it too, came just the same.

The best I can figure, I turned fifty thirty-three thousand feet somewhere over Albuquerque, New Mexico. Strangely enough, I have to admit that I didn't feel any different or look any different. I didn't have a sudden urge to climb out of my plane seat and into a rocking chair. In fact, I felt pretty good. Fifty arrived without incident and I was still myself.

So far, being fifty has been a lot of fun. In fact, I think I really like being fifty. I am healthy, have a great family, and lots of great friends. I live in a great community, have a great job and am blessed in so many ways.

I actually look forward to spending the next ten years as a fifty-something-year-old.

So I guess it is true that age is only a state of mind and that you are only as old as you feel. It seems that life only gets better. I can't wait to see what my sixties will bring. Well, then again, maybe I can wait a little!

Part III

On Nature

LET HEAVEN
AND NATURE SING

Twirling Squirrels

For those of us who enjoy feeding the birds in our yards, squirrels can sometimes become annoying pests. The clever little critters can figure out how to raid even the most sophisticated of bird feeders, leaving nothing behind but hulls and a few scattered seed for our feathered friends. I have tried unsuccessfully to deter the squirrels from eating at my bird feeders using baffles, poles, and screens. I even invested in a couple of squirrel feeders a while back, thinking it would give them their own private dining area. The additional feeders just caused the squirrel population in my yard to multiply, making the problem worse.

That is why I was interested in a bird feeder I saw at a store a few weeks ago. The words "guaranteed squirrel proof" were written across the front of the box in large letters. There was also a cute cartoon picture of a squirrel wearing aviator goggles, preparing to sail through the air in the opposite direction of the feeder. I decided I would give it a try.

When I returned home, I pulled the new feeder from the carton. To my surprise, an electrical cord fell out of the box with the feeder. I read the directions and discovered the cord was used to charge the batteries in a small motor at the base of the feeder.

When a squirrel touched one of the feeder's metal perches, its weight would activate the motor, causing the perches to spin. The object, twirl the little seed thief around in circles until it flips off the feeder.

For about ten seconds, I thought about taking the bird feeder back. After all, twirling unsuspecting squirrels around in the air and having them fall to the ground seems a little bit mean.

But then I fell to temptation. Curiosity got the best of me and I wanted to see this thing in action.

I set up the new bird feeder outside my living room window near a line of trees, a popular hangout for the neighborhood squirrels. I figured this would be a great place to put it to the test. It was also in an area surrounded by soft landing spots, necessary according to the directions, to keep the squirrels from being injured. Squirrels, like cats, have the uncanny ability to always land on their feet when they fall from a distance.

It was late in the afternoon that day when I heard Mousie, my tiny Yorkshire terrier, barking at something outside the window from her own perch on the living room couch. I went to check. Sure enough, the first squirrel victim had ventured to where the new feeder was hanging in the yard. I stood very still as I watched out the window, anxious to see what would happen next.

The cautious squirrel slowly made its way up the side of the pine tree.

Next, it inched out onto the thin wrought iron hook holding the feeder balancing as if it were a tightrope.

It took a few minutes for the squirrel to figure out the long clear cylinder holding the bird seed. Gradually, gaining confidence, it began a very slow slide, head first, down the plastic tube. When the squirrel reached the bottom of the tube, there were only the three metal perches for it to grab in order to keep from falling off the feeder. The squirrel grabbed one of them and the motorized perches immediately began to spin around like helicopter blades, causing the squirrel to go in circles while holding on for dear life with its little front feet.

After about halfway into the second full twirl, the dizzy squirrel was slung from the feeder and through the air, much to Mousie's amusement.

When the squirrel hit the ground, I ran to the window to see its reaction. The squirrel sat up straight and looked around, as if it were trying to figure out what had happened. Then, believe it or not, after regaining its wits, the tenacious little squirrel climbed back up the tree and onto the feeder and went for a second whirl.

Most of the veteran squirrels in our yard have caught on to the twirling birdfeeder now. They are happy to scoff up the extra seed that drop from the feeder as our feathered friends finally dine in peace. However, there still seems to be a steady supply of newcomers to the yard, naïve squirrels that test out the new feeder for themselves.

The squirrel-twirling bird feeder has now been relocated to the front of the house so our parrot, Mildred, can also watch the action. We always know when a squirrel has been twirled. Mousie lets out a bark and Mildred follows with a laugh and a loud "Yee-Haw!"

The Perfect Snowfall

Last weekend, we experienced the first snowfall of the year and it was nothing short of perfect.

Since it snowed on Saturday, it did not interfere with school schedules or create a future need for the always dreaded "make up" day for students and staff.

The snowflakes were big and fluffy. Not only did they make for a beautiful sight as they floated gently from the sky, they were just the right size to catch on your tongue if you happened to venture outdoors and be so inclined.

There was also enough snow to cover the ground. This provided the opportunity to make some nice winter pictures and for youngsters to roll a few snowballs or build a small snowman in the yard.

Most importantly, however, the snow had all but disappeared the following morning. It stuck around just long enough to boost the local economy through bread and milk sales and to make for some interesting conversation and a thoroughly entertaining day.

Come Sunday morning, the sun was bright and the sky was a brilliant Carolina blue. Life quickly returned to normal and, with the exception of a few sparse white patches on the ground that quickly melted away, one would have never even known that it had snowed.

Like I said, it was definitely the perfect snowfall.

Ants with Attitude

In 1954, a horror flick was released about an army of giant man-eating ants that were threatening to take over civilization. The name of the movie was Them! The king-sized ants had mutated from small ordinary ants as a result of an atomic bomb test in the New Mexico desert. You knew when the giant ants were about to attack. A shrill, eerie noise would fill the air, followed by a moment of deathly quiet. Then suddenly the gigantic ants would appear, causing people to panic and flee for their lives.

Of course, what made the movie scary was the thought of a tiny little ant mutating into a monster ant that could actually attack people. After all, ants were small, harmless creatures. The only trouble an ant might cause you was an occasional visit to your sugar bowl or family picnic.

When I was a kid, I never thought twice about kicking an ant hill. Whenever you kicked one, it was fun to watch the tiny ants scramble and try to regroup after the unexpected jolt to their home. Back then, ants were nice insects.

They never retaliated and tried to get you back.

Then along came the fire ant, and everything changed.

Fire ants are quickly taking over here in southeastern North Carolina. I have decided that fire ants are simply miniature versions of the monster ants in the movie Them! Don't let their tiny size fool you. Fire ants are vicious and ornery creatures.

What a fire ant lacks in size, it makes up in attitude.

At least those Hollywood ants played fair. They signaled a warning of their impending attack. They were also big so you could see them coming and they attacked one on one. Fire ants do not play fair.

Fire ants give you no warning. They are sneaky little insects that live under the ground and out of sight. They build their homes in tall grasses and in your flower beds. Unless you are constantly looking down for them, they are hard to spot. Generally, by the time you are attacked by fire ants, you never even saw them coming.

Fire ants do not attack one on one.

They gang up on you and they attack as a team. Each tiny member of a fire ant team can wield a bite that causes a powerful sting. The sting slowly turns into a steady burning sensation that can last for days. I guess that is how the nasty little insects got their name.

If you happen to step on a fire ant mound, it is an experience you are not likely to soon forget. An army of tiny soldier ants will immediately swarm to the surface of the ground to take out whoever happens to be standing the closest by. It doesn't matter to a fire ant whether you were the actual culprit or not.

Needless to say, these days, I would think twice about kicking an ant hill. Fire ants must love the heat and dry conditions we have experienced this summer because their sandy homes have popped up everywhere. I have developed a survival skill of looking down as I walk in my yard to avoid the ant mounds. I also try to memorize their general locations.

The other day, I was out watering the plants, trying my best to steer clear of the fire ants. Things were going along fine until I moved close to the flower pots on the sidewalk. I began to feel a sudden stinging sensation on my left ankle. I looked down and sure enough, I was standing in the middle of a huge mound of fire ants.

They were swarming across my sneaker straight toward my bare ankle.

Kicking off my shoes, I ran as fast as I could and stuck both my feet in the fishpond. Fortunately, they only got in a few bites.

In the movie Them! there is a professor who tries to formulate a plan to kill the giant mutant ants. That professor reminds me of Mike, who has his own obsession with exterminating fire ants. Getting rid of fire ants is tough. Mike has tried granules, sprays, liquids, and powders. He once even tried setting them on fire, saying the only way to fight fire is with fire. However the tenacious little ants always seem to come back, only in a different location.

The last fire ant colony I reported was on the sidewalk, close to the front porch. Mike took a canister of insecticide and sprinkled some of the white powder on the mound.

The next day, the ants were gone.

The following day, I discovered they had relocated about three feet further up the sidewalk. Yes, right next to my flower pots where I experienced their revenge.

Maybe a cold winter will slow those ants with an attitude down. Until then, watch your step whenever you go outside for a walk. You won't hear a shrill, eerie noise to warn you and you won't see them, unless you are looking down.

But rest assured they are still out there.

Just try your best not to step on them!

Anticipation of Snow

My mother used to say one of the most exciting things about going on a vacation is the feeling of anticipation as you prepare for the trip. It is the feeling you get inside when you look forward to something very special, she would tell me.

Perhaps that same idea holds true for Southerners when it comes to the anticipation of a significant snowfall. We don't get to see those very often here in southeastern North Carolina.

More often, we are simply teased with forecasts of possible snow in neighboring counties to our north and west.

So when the weather forecast last Monday called for five to eight inches of snow in our area, one couldn't help but feel excited in anticipation of seeing a sight we seldom get to see. What's more, it was reported that the snow was coming as a result of cold air from the north meeting moisture from the south, which usually does bring us our significant snow.

On Monday afternoon, we were placed under a winter weather advisory.

Updated weather forecasts appeared in the news and those reports were shared through excited chatter on social media. Many, including myself, prepared by making a run to the grocery store for milk and bread in anticipation.

I have to admit I went for milk and bread even though we had milk and bread. Why? It was all part of the excitement of anticipation. Going to the store for milk and bread is what we southerners do when snow is predicted.

Also, there is always the chance you will run into friends and neighbors who are there for the very same reason, and sharing the excitement adds to the anticipation.

I guess my mom was right. Anticipation is one of the best parts of things that we deem special in our lives, whether it be a welcomed vacation or a beautiful snowfall.

Hummingbirds
Bring Simple Pleasure

During the past few weeks, three hummingbirds finally discovered the feeders we have had hanging in our yard since late last spring. It has been fun watching them as they maneuver around the feeders, like tiny, feathered helicopters. When they are not feeding, the three little birds rest on the limbs of an old oak tree in the backyard.

We have noticed that one of the hummingbirds, an aggressive little fellow we call Bandit, chases the other two, who we named HB and Buzz, away from the feeders. However, the two more timid birds do get an occasional drink of the red nectar, whenever Bandit lets down his guard.

This weekend, Bandit chased little Buzz, the smallest of the three hummingbirds, through the open door on our back porch. The frightened little bird flew around in circles on the high ceiling, confused and unable to figure out how to get back out the door. Finally, the exhausted little bird flew lower and then suddenly landed gently in Mike's hand.

Mike took the little green bird out the porch door to release him. Amazingly, the tiny bird just sat on my husband's hand for several minutes resting, allowing me to get a picture of a very unusual sight. Then, with a gentle lift, the little bird flew away, buzzing back to a branch of the old oak tree.

It wasn't long before Bandit, HB, and little Buzz were back to business as usual, entertaining us and fighting over the feeders.

It's funny how such simple things in life can bring us so much pleasure.

The Blind Possum

Weasel, my old barn cat and her kittens were crossing the pasture the other day. I glanced over and saw what appeared to be an extra cat lagging behind the group. As they approached, I realized the extra cat was actually an opossum. It was still daylight and I thought it strange since opossums are nocturnal animals, and it is a little unusual to see one out of the cover of the woods at that time of day.

I ventured a little closer to get a better look. The opossum was sniffing around on the ground and acted as though he didn't see me. That is when I saw his eyes.

They were both completely clouded and white. If he wasn't completely blind, this poor creature was obviously severely visually challenged. He was using his nose to find his way around. He was very skinny and I was somewhat surprised that the animal had made it this long in the woods without becoming someone else's dinner.

I felt so sorry for him that I went back to the car to retrieve a few leftover hushpuppies I was taking home from my lunch at Bruce and Mickey's. I tossed one to him. He must have really liked it because he scoffed up the hushpuppy and began sniffing around for more. As much as I hated to part with them, I decided to throw him my remaining two hushpuppies I had saved from lunch. He stuffed both of those in his mouth, turned, and slowly began to make his way back through the fence and into the woods.

Needless to say, I felt like I had done a good deed. You see, I have a soft spot in my heart for opossums. I have found that most people think opossums, or possums, as we call them down South, are just disgusting, hideously ugly creatures with triangular faces and ratlike tails who eat out of garbage cans. Although I will admit that they do eat out of garbage cans from time to time, I don't think possums are disgusting or ugly. In fact, I think they are kind of cute.

Most people would never believe a possum could actually win a beauty contest. But that is simply not true. I used to have my own pet possum and although she didn't actually win, she was first runner-up in a national beauty contest for possums. When people find this out, they want to know how in the world I ended up with a possum as a pet. My parents blamed that on my sixth grade teacher, Mrs. Ruth Aderholt.

Mrs. Aderholt was one of those teachers who made school fun. One day, she had something strange sitting on the corner of her desk in the classroom. It was square, about the size of a bread box and was completely covered with a light blue towel. Mrs. Aderholt told us that there was something under that towel and that we should spend the morning listening and thinking about what it might be.

Just before lunch, she passed out small slips of paper. Everyone was asked to write down our guess as to what might be hidden beneath the towel. I remember guessing a hamster because I thought I had heard faint scratching noises earlier in the morning and whatever was under the towel appeared to be about the size of my hamster's cage at home.

After lunch, Mrs. Aderholt read all the guesses aloud to the class. Some were funny. Some were ridiculous. But none were correct, according to Mrs. Aderholt. She removed the towel and there in a cage on the corner of her desk was a small baby opossum. She told us her name was Opie and that she had fallen from a tree as a tiny, helpless, hairless baby. Mrs. Aderholt used a medicine dropper to nurse her and she was quite tame.

For the remainder of the school year, I would walk to Mrs. Aderholt's house on Saturdays, to play with Opie and help clean out her cage. At the end of the school year, Mrs. Aderholt called my parents and asked if she could give me Opie. So that is how I came to have a possum for a pet.

One day, we heard that there was going to be a beauty contest for possums at the National Hollering Contest in Spivey's Corner, NC. The decision was made to enter Opie. She wore a bright blue bow around her neck. Unfortunately, Opie took second place to another possum wearing a gown and granny hat. I still think she was the prettiest possum at the show.

By the way, I continue to return to the pasture around dusk each afternoon, checking on that old blind possum. I have even taken a few hushpuppies and tossed them over the fence, in hopes he will find them. So far there has been no sign of him. However, I have noticed that in the mornings those hushpuppies are usually gone. I realize that there are a lot of hungry critters out there in the woods.

However, I would like to believe those Bruce and Mickey's hushpuppies were sniffed out and devoured by my new possum friend.

Song Bird Symphony

I saw a robin in my yard the other morning. He was hopping around and pecking at the ground, no doubt looking for a worm and insect breakfast. I have always heard that seeing your first robin of the New Year is the very first sign that spring has arrived. I have already observed several other indicators that signal spring is definitely here.

The Bradford pears are in full bloom now and the dogwood trees are in the early stages, as their blooms are just beginning to open. The azaleas and other flowers have started to bud. Winter's dry, brown grass is beginning to turn a brilliant green. My white car is a pale shade of yellow from the pollen that has filled the air.

The days are growing longer, and people are starting to spend more time outdoors in their yards.

There are other changes that have occurred as spring makes her debut in southeastern North Carolina. The weather has changed with the morning temperatures cool, the daytime temperatures growing warmer, and the evening temperatures cooling back off again. Throughout the day, a welcome breeze often blows to help us gradually acclimate to the new warmer temperatures. The long awaited strawberry blooms are now visible in the fields, a sign that strawberry season is around the corner and that before too long, we can once again indulge in shortcake, topped with whipped cream and mounds of local fresh ripe berries.

Early spring also brings us another special gift. Each morning, we are given the opportunity to attend a free musical concert sponsored by Mother Nature herself. There are few things more beautiful than the song bird symphony that occurs at daybreak on an early spring morning. Lately, I have gotten up extra early just to experience it. With coffee mug in hand, I take my designated seat in the audience in a rocking chair on my front porch. There is usually a morning chill in the air and it is extremely quiet, with little of the noise you hear throughout the day.

As dawn begins to break out of the darkness, the sky transforms to a silver-gray color. At almost the very second the sky lightens, a single bird awakes and begins to sing and chatter, letting others know it is time to get up and start the day. Soon after that solo begins, other birds begin to join in the chorus, creating harmony from all different directions until finally the air fills with the music of song birds, music that rivals any symphony orchestra I have ever heard.

Before we know it, this glorious season will become yet another memory and hot summer days will be upon us.

So take some time in the spring to enjoy the flowers, the birds, the green grass, and the beautiful trees. Enjoy the strawberries and warm breezy days.

And if you get a chance, get up a little early and take advantage of your free admission to the song bird symphony at daybreak.

I am sure you will find it well worth your time.

Baby Birds

Rarely do I see a baby bird in midsummer. That is why I was somewhat surprised the other day to discover a baby mockingbird sitting inside one of the links in my chain-link fence. His mother was perched on the top of the fence rail about ten yards away. She was making quite a fuss, too, even with the large berry she had stuffed inside her beak.

It would appear that this mother bird had her little one out for one of his daily lessons on how to survive in the wild. My presence was obviously creating a disruption.

I am not certain, but I am guessing that the baby bird's mother is one of the two mockingbirds that have staked their claim to the old oak tree in our backyard. These vocal birds sing beautiful, almost operatic, songs throughout the day. After snapping a few pictures, I left the baby bird alone so mother could get back to her instruction. I did go back and check on him periodically though, just to make sure he was okay. I even gave the little fellow a name—Link.

I love baby birds. When I was a kid, if I found one I would take it home always thinking I was doing a good deed. Then I would get the usual lecture about how you are not supposed to touch baby birds.

The mother and father bird are always somewhere close by, I was told, just like the one vigilantly watching over little Link.

Baby birds need their parents to take care of them and teach them how to survive on their own.

On one occasion, however, I found a baby bird that had no parents.

It was a tiny starling and he was all alone. I brought him home and put him in a shoebox containing a makeshift nest I constructed of pine straw. I named the little bird Oliver, as in Oliver Twist, because he was an orphan.

Once he got of some size, I transferred Oliver to an old parakeet cage. Since he had no parents, I tried my best to teach him how to be a bird. I had my brothers gather bugs and worms for him. I would feed those to him, along with a little cat food, from the end of a toothpick.

After Oliver developed his pin feathers, I would take him out in the yard for flying lessons. He would practice flying each day. One sunny morning, when he was strong enough to fly a little distance, my brother Derb took Oliver outside and threw him up in the air. Oliver flew up and away, high into the trees. That is where Derb said birds were supposed to live. Although I knew my brother was right, I still cried and cried that day.

The next morning, I got up early and went outside. You can only imagine how surprised I was when ole Oliver flew down from the tree, where he had spent the night, and landed gently on my shoulder. He was hungry and wanted something to eat.

That is when I realized that what I hadn't done was to teach Oliver how to find his own food.

The little starling continued living outdoors in the trees with the other birds, but he would fly down and land on my shoulder or fly through an open back door to a chair at the kitchen table whenever he was hungry. Occasionally, he would fly down and land on the neighbors, too. He was seen riding on Al Prewitt's head while he was cutting grass on his riding lawn mower. And once, he made a spectacle of himself at Mrs. Weeks' garden party, bombarding all the ladies in their fancy hats and white gloves as they were having tea on the patio.

Thank goodness that Link, the baby mockingbird holding tight to our backyard fence, will grow up in the wild under the direction of his real parents. I hope little Link learns his lessons well.

I hope he learns how to fly high up into the trees.

I hope he learns how to find his own insects, bugs, berries, and seeds.

I hope he learns how to keep his distance from cats, dogs, and even humans.

I hope he learns how to build a safe nest for his family.

And I hope he learns to sing just like his parents.

I look forward to the day when little Link grows up to take his place in the mockingbird choir.

Avian Acrobats

I have been thoroughly entertained this summer by three avian acrobats. These airborne gymnasts are tiny hummingbirds, each no bigger than my thumb. They zoom through the air with the greatest of ease.

With seemingly little effort, they fly up, down, backwards, and forwards.

They hover in place like tiny helicopters. Periodically, you may even see one break loose and perform a loop-de-loop in midair.

Hummingbirds naturally frequent places where nectar-producing flowers grow. But they also visit yards where people provide special feeders to attract them in the summer. It has only been in the past few years that I have placed a hummingbird feeder in my yard during the summer months.

Until then, I didn't know what I was missing.

Watching these spirited little birds can provide hours of enjoyment. My hummingbird feeder is located just off our backyard deck. That way, I am able to observe their antics from my kitchen window. Surprisingly, there are approximately 340 varieties of hummingbirds.

The three that visit my feeder are distinguishably different in both color and size. They even have different personalities.

There is a small shy one who likes to perch on top of the hook that holds the feeder. Not only is it smaller, it is much lighter in color than the other two. The second one is a medium-green with a gray throat and belly marked with darker gray spots, resembling a dove. When it comes to feeding, this little fellow is all business.

The third one, mostly darker green with a black head and a ruby-red throat, is larger and much more aggressive.

It tends to boss the other two around.

Hummingbirds consume almost half of their body weight in

food a day. During daylight hours, you are sure to see one of the three at the feeder every few minutes. I have discovered that store-bought hummingbird food can be rather expensive. However, you really don't need to purchase packaged hummingbird food to enjoy hummingbirds in your yard. A simple mixture of sugar and water does the trick. I use one part granulated sugar to four parts water.

Then I boil it on the stove or in the microwave and allow it to cool before filling the feeder.

This helps reduce the growth of bacteria and mildew in the feeder. Since the birds are already attracted to the red plastic parts of the feeder, there is no need to add artificial color to the water, which is probably better for the birds anyway.

Hummingbirds are migratory birds.

They spend their winters in the warmer climates of Mexico and Central America.

In late spring, many hummingbirds return to spend the summer here with us, just like the three visitors in my backyard. In a few weeks, those of us with feeders know we will have to take them down. With the onset of fall, the hummingbirds must begin their migration back to their winter home if they are to survive. I know I will soon be wishing the three little visitors to my backyard a safe flight as they make nature's journey.

I find solace in the fact that I have always heard hummingbirds have good memories. They can remember the locations where they found abundant food and often return to the same place each season. I do hope these three tiny aerial acrobats will not forget the time they spent in my backyard this summer. I will definitely be looking forward to their return again next year.

The Baby Wrens

I heard a faint, familiar chirping sound on our front porch. I looked around and saw a house wren perched on a side rail. The little bird had a tiny worm dangling from both sides of its beak. When it saw me, the little brown bird made a sudden dive into a nearby geranium plant. *Baby birds!* I thought.

Then I panicked. Just the day before, I had stuck a small decorative American flag down into that same potted plant. I remember having to jab the little flagpole down between the leaves several times to get it deep enough in the soil to make it secure. Slowly I pulled back the leaves of the geranium, praying that I had not accidentally stabbed the baby birds with the flagpole. I was quite relieved to find three baby house wrens safely asleep in their nest.

I called Mike to come look at the baby birds in the geranium plant. I told him how lucky they were because I had come so close to stabbing them with the little flagpole. "You think that's bad," he said, peering into the plant at the tiny birds. "I've been watering them every day with a garden hose."

We gently removed the flag from the pot and we stopped watering the geranium plant. It wasn't long before the three little wrens grew strong enough to leave the nest. Early one morning, we watched the babies hop and flutter across our front yard, trying out their tiny wings. The mother and father bird flew to a nearby crepe myrtle tree and did what mother and father birds do when their babies leave the nest. They began to chirp loudly to get the baby birds to follow them toward safe cover. With the exception of one slight detour into our open garage, the baby birds obeyed and headed straight to the nearby tree line.

Today the little wren nest in our geranium plant looks empty. But as Andy Griffith explained to Opie during one of my favorite episodes, perhaps that is why our "trees seem nice and full."

A Snowy Day

Last week's snowfall brought a beautiful quietness to our small community. For a while that snowy morning, I stood on my front porch with a friend and just watched it snow. We drank hot coffee and we talked. Mostly, we talked about the snow and how beautiful it was falling gently from the sky. We commented on the size of the snowflakes as they changed from large flakes to smaller ones and then back to larger ones again.

Later that morning, I looked out my kitchen window. A fresh blanket of white snow had covered the ground. I thought about being a kid on a day like this one. I remembered all the excitement and joy created by a snowy day. I think there is something about snow that brings out the kid and the joy in all of us.

Years ago, weather forecasting was not as sophisticated as it is today, so sometimes snow came as an unexpected surprise. I recall the excitement of waking up in the morning to discover it had snowed overnight. You could hear squeals of delight and shouts of "It's snowing!" echoing all throughout the house. The first order of business was to turn on the television and tune in the local radio station to listen for school cancellation notices.

Back then, there was no such thing as the continual scrolling of this kind of information you now see at the bottom of the television screen. You would have to wait patiently for your school district's name to be read in alphabetical order. If there were going to be a delay, the school system had some kind of special schedule. There was schedule A and schedule B, which always seemed confusing even to the adults. Of course, what the kids were always hoping to hear was the announcement that school was closed for the entire day. We would cross our fingers and hope. The minutes spent waiting for our school district's announcement would seem like hours. When news finally came that school was cancelled for the day, we would dance around the room and jump for joy.

After breakfast, we would scramble to get into our snow clothes. This took a little doing. The attire consisted of layer upon layer of socks, pants, shirts, and sweaters. All these clothes were then concealed under a large heavy coat causing you to resemble something that looked very much like the Michelin man. The outfit was finished off with boots, a pair of thick gloves, and a knitted hat. We called our knitted hats toboggans, even though I have since been told that a toboggan is actually a sled. Some of our toboggans were actually masks designed to completely cover your face, leaving only a small hole for each of your eyes and one for your mouth.

After getting dressed, we would hurry down to the basement and pull out our old red and brown Radio Flyer, the one sled that was shared by all three kids. Gathering any additional equipment we needed in the form of bread pans and large pots from the kitchen, we would head outdoors for a full day of slipping and sliding in the snow with our friends.

When you first stepped outside, it was like something magical had happened to the world. Everything looked so different and clean. Everything was so peaceful and calm. And it was really quiet. The only sound heard was the crunching of the snow beneath our feet. We would try our best not to make tracks in the front yard so it would look good for the pictures that we knew would be forthcoming. With our equipment in hand, we would make our way up the street.

There was a nearby road in our neighborhood that provided the perfect sledding hill. This is where everyone flocked with their sleds, pots and pans to spend the day. It was the perfect sledding hill because it was really steep with a slight, steady curve all the way down. Starting at the top of the hill, the ride down took the good part of two minutes from start to finish.

It was a long, slippery walk back up to the top, but the ride was well worth it. There would be races and sledding contests all day long. Hours were spent playing and sledding, with an occasional friendly snowball fight just for fun.

When we finally returned home, we were usually exhausted. The warmth of the house would cause our hands and face to sting and tingle. Exchanging our wet clothes for a set of dry ones, we would head to the kitchen. There would be a saucepan of homemade hot chocolate, simmering on the stove, to help us warm up. Later, we would make a large bowl of snow cream out of snow, sugar, vanilla extract and a little milk. To me, it was better than any store-bought ice cream. After resting up a while, we would bundle back up and head back outdoors to continue to slip and slide with our friends until dark.

I am grown now and my ambition to slip and slide all day in the snow no longer exists. On a snowy day, I am now very much content to just stay inside next to a cozy fire and simply watch the snow out the window, or better yet, to stand for a while on my front porch, drink hot coffee, and discuss the snowfall with a good friend. Regardless, I still get that same feeling of joy that I had as a kid whenever it snows. I hope I always will.

Feathered Friends

I opened my front door and discovered two Canadian geese standing in a tiny fishpond located in our yard. They were standing so still that at first I thought they were two plastic statues—you know the kind that people buy to decorate their lawns. I figured Mike must have put them in the fishpond as a joke when I wasn't looking.

However, as I moved closer to see them, they also moved. I am not sure who was startled the most, the geese or me. These were not plastic statues. These geese were very much alive! I stood staring at the two beautiful creatures thinking that they were probably displaced wildlife, just another part of the ongoing tragedy of losing the lake. I felt really sorry for them and decided to go back quietly into the house and let them enjoy the hot day cooling off in the tiny pond.

I am not really sure exactly when they left or where they went, but I noticed the geese were gone very late in the afternoon. I went out in the yard to look at the little pond where they had spent part of their day. I gasped! In a few short hours, my new feathered friends, which by now I had named Dick and Frances, had uprooted and eaten all of my precious water lilies, torn up my newly planted water iris, destroyed a brand new birdfeeder, and eaten all the birdseed.

They had also, very obviously, decided to turn our driveway and sidewalk into a goose restroom. Thank goodness, I thought, there were no goldfish in the pond because they would have no doubt become sushi. When Mike saw the mess, he commented under his breath about how lucky the geese were that it wasn't hunting season.

The next morning, I woke to find the two geese once again standing in the little fishpond, no doubt ready for another destructive day. Dick and Frances, I thought to myself, would have to go. The only question was how to do it.

I obviously do not believe in Mike's tactics for goose removal so I had to come up with a few of my own. First, I thought I would start with the easiest, most non-confrontational strategy I could think of—to simply ask them politely to leave. I walked behind them, gently "shooing" and telling them to go away, hoping they would leave my yard on their own accord. They waddled in front of me making a large circle around the yard.

We all three ended up right back to the same spot in front of the pond. Frustrated, I decided my second tactic would have to be more aggressive. I flapped my arms and ran toward them squawking loudly thinking they would think I was a bigger goose, get scared and fly away.

This actually backfired. The larger of the two geese turned and ran back at me hissing and I got scared and ran away. My third strategy, making loud noises clanging pots and pans together, didn't work either. They actually seemed to enjoy it. And turning the dog out on the lawn didn't seem to bother them at all. Mousie only weighs three pounds so I guess she was not viewed as a major threat.

Eventually, I gave up realizing Dick and Frances are simply trying to make it through some long, hot summer days. Like the rest of us, they miss the lake and are waiting for the water so they can return to their rightful environment.

This new temporary environment is not their first choice for a home, but a last resort. And I am sure living in a tiny fishpond, in such a cramped and limited space, isn't that much fun for them either. They probably have some serious questions about their new landlords, too! Hopefully, before too long, Dick and Frances will be back swimming on Hope Mills Lake where they can spread their wings and spend long, lazy days enjoying the good life. We can watch and enjoy the beautiful scenery they create for our community.

So for now, Mike and I will anxiously await the day when Dick and Frances can upgrade from our tiny fishpond to a much bigger, more beautiful watery home. Until then, our feathered friends are more than welcome to spend a little time each day cooling off in our tiny pond.

Winter Is for the Birds

Wild birds add color and music to our surroundings. They are also interesting and fun to watch. That is why I, like so many others, enjoy feeding the wild birds that visit our yard throughout the year.

Feeding wild birds during the cold winter months is especially important. In the winter, wild birds have more difficulty finding sources of food. Their natural diet of insects and bugs, abundant during the warmer months of the year, become scarce in cold weather. Nuts and seeds can get buried deep beneath leaves, straw, snow, and ice. Feeding wild birds during the winter time not only supplements their natural diet, it also helps to increase their chances for survival.

You can readily purchase many types of bird feeders and bird food at local stores. Feeders can range from fairly inexpensive tube vessels to more decorative and elaborate models. Likewise, you can purchase simple wild bird seed to fill your feeders or more pricey mixtures of seed designed to attract particular types of birds to your yard.

Feeding wild birds doesn't have to be complicated or costly. Homemade bird food and bird feeders work quite well and can be relatively cheap and easy to make. Creating a homemade bird café in your yard can be both rewarding and educational. You will be provided many opportunities to learn more about the different varieties of birds and their habits.

Pine cones make great homemade bird feeders and more than likely, you can readily find them somewhere in your neighborhood. Larger pine cones, with wide pedals, make the best feeders. To make a pine cone feeder, just stuff the cone with a mixture of finely crushed low-sodium crackers, bread crumbs or cornmeal mixed with crunchy peanut butter. Use a piece of wire or string to hang the pine cone from a Shepard's hook or in a tree about five feet off the ground.

The smaller birds, especially the nuthatches, finches, and warblers, will love your pine cone feeder. One warning though, you may want to make more than one. The birds can become territorial and will fight over rights to just one feeder.

Another easy and relatively inexpensive way to feed the birds during the winter is to put suet out for them. You can request suet, or animal fat, from the meat department at most local grocery stores. If they have it available, you can usually get the suet free of charge.

Suet is a great source of energy for wild birds during the winter months. Cut the suet into small pieces and stuff it into one-inch holes drilled in a piece of wood. Attach a wire, string or small chain to the top for a hanger. Cedar works great for this type of feeder because it will not rot.

An even easier method is to place the suet in a mesh bag, like an onion, grapefruit or orange bag, and put it out for the birds. The bag is tied at the top and hung from a tree about five feet off the ground.

If you choose to purchase bird seed, one of the best choices is black oil sunflower seed. Nearly all birds eat black oil sunflower seed so it allows you to feed a wide variety of birds. I like to supplement my homemade bird food with a few feeders filled with black oil sunflower seeds.

Birds have a way of fluttering into our hearts throughout the year. Helping our feathered friends survive the cold winter months is one simple way that we can ensure a brighter spring.

The Wreath Babies

Early this spring, we noticed a small bird nest on top of one of our front door wreaths. The little straw nest did not contain any eggs. We debated over the mess that would surely come with baby birds, but decided to leave it alone and let nature take her course.

The following day, there was a tiny bright blue egg inside the little nest.

A day later, there were two.

By the end of the week, there were five tiny blue eggs in the little straw nest.

I learned that the birds building their home in our wreath were a pair of house finches.

We limited using the front door as much as possible in order to keep from disturbing the mother bird as she sat on her eggs. We even placed a sign on the door asking visitors to ring the doorbell instead of knocking.

Occasionally, I would take a picture or video clip of the nest with the little blue eggs to share with my friends on Facebook. The mother and father bird would patiently watch me from the edge of the roof. Then one morning, we could hear tiny chirping sounds through the front door.

Five baby birds, we affectionately called our wreath babies, were hatched and snuggled in the nest. The parent birds were busy flying back and forth to the nest, taking turns feeding them. The five wreath babies grew quickly.

A few weeks later, when I opened the door, I saw all five baby birds fly from the nest at once. The tiny brown birds looked as though they had been flying all of their lives. Later that afternoon, we spotted one of the wreath babies sitting quietly in a nearby Crepe Myrtle tree. With a feeling of satisfaction, we cleaned the front porch and the door wreath that had served as home to the little bird family. Afterwards, you would have never known that five baby birds had been raised on our front porch.

Life was back to normal, and we could finally use our front door without any worry. One week later, however, a brand new nest appeared on top of that very same wreath on our front porch.

Here we go again!

Part IV

FUR, FEATHERS, AND FINS

Mildred

Mildred is in rare form this morning. To tell you the truth, she is getting on my nerves. She has reminded me to take out the trash five or six times. She has asked me what I am doing eight times in a row. I just ignore her.

"What is your problem?" she yells over and over.

I continue to ignore her.

Next she gets angry and turns her attention to the dog. "Hey, Mousie! Come here!" Mousie ignores her. She gives an ear-piercing whistle. "Mousie! Come here!" she demands again. This time Mousie reluctantly obeys and walks across the room to look at her.

Mildred scolds, "You are a bad dog! A bad, bad dog!"

Mousie puts her tiny head down and returns in shame to her little bed in the laundry room. Mildred continues on with her annoying behavior. At the top of her lungs, she begins to whistle the theme song from The Andy Griffith Show, adding a few of her own notes here and there just to make it sound different. This goes on and on until I can stand it no longer.

From the chair in my office I finally yell, "Mildred, hush!"

"Mildred, hush!" she yells back sarcastically imitating my voice and then erupts into a roar of laughter that sounds exactly like my husband, Mike. This causes me to burst out laughing.

Such begins a typical day in the Waring household.

Mildred is our eight-year-old African Gray Parrot. I named her after my eighth grade Math teacher, Ms. Mildred Crawley. Everything in our home basically revolves around Mildred. Mildred rules the roost. Yes, she can be aggravating at times, but we still love her. You can't help but love Mildred. She adds so much pleasure to our lives simply by being around. We don't have to go out on the town or to the movies to be entertained. We have Mildred.

She is our live-in comic and our 24/7 entertainment center. She never hesitates to tell you what she thinks and she keeps us constantly laughing and talking.

There is a never a dull moment with Mildred around the house.

"Guess what Mildred just told me?" Mike will ask.

"You won't believe what I heard Mildred say!" I will tell Mike. Sometimes I call him at work just to recount Mildred's latest antics. No matter how busy he may be, he always wants to hear.

Mildred and Mike share the den.

Her cage is strategically placed in front of a large window so she can keep an eye on what is going in the front yard while still being able to see the television and watch her favorite shows.

A small birdfeeder hangs in a tree right outside her window so she can have conversations with her little bird friends who stop by to visit her on a regular basis.

Perched in her cage, Mildred keeps an eye on things for us.

She whistles loudly to let us know when someone pulls in the driveway. She barks like a dog when they get out of their car. Mildred is our personal Feathered First Alert System and she never hesitates to call the dogs if she needs back up.

Over the years, Mildred seems to have developed her own personal fan club.

People actually come to our house to visit Mildred, not us. You never know what she is going to say or when she is going to say it. She has an extensive vocabulary and can amazingly combine words into complete sentences and sentences into paragraphs.

She loves to watch The Price is Right and screams with delight when someone wins a prize.

She yells, "Swing batter, batter, batter!" when she and Mike are engrossed in an Atlanta Braves game. She exclaims "Merry Christmas! Ho! Ho! Ho!" when someone plugs in the Christmas tree during the holidays.

Mildred loves to imitate the ring of the phone just to see if she can fool us into running to answer it. Sometimes we miss telephone calls because we think it may be Mildred up to her games. When the phone actually does ring, she immediately answers with "Hello? Okay, Bye!"

Mildred can sing opera, but not very well. She occasionally demands peanuts, cherries, and bananas. Unfortunately, she also knows a few words we wish she didn't know.

Even though I raised Mildred from a chick, for the most part, she is now Mike's bird.

She only mildly tolerates me. When Mike leaves to go to work each morning, he rings a brass bell that hangs on the wall by the door going out to the garage. Mildred rings the bell in her cage back in response. I guess that is how they say good-bye to each other. Before he closes the door, he tells her he loves her and she tells him she loves him back.

I tell Mike that I never imagined that he, the epitome of the Southern sportsman, could ever get so attached to a bird. He tells me that he never imagined a bird could be so intelligent and have such personality.

Yes, our lives are definitely richer for having Miss Mildred around the house.

Well, I guess I better go.

The phone just rang. Or then again, "Was that Mildred?"

Meagan

I received a very special card in the mail. It was from the Fayetteville Animal Protection Society notifying me that a donation had been made by my cousin Janice Melton in memory of Meagan, a beloved dog.

My eyes welled up with tears. Janice truly understands how much it hurts to lose a family pet.

I believe that all dogs go to heaven. Recently, a new angel arrived in heaven by the name of Meagan. Meagan was our Yorkshire terrier.

She was five pounds of furry, unconditional love and joy.

Meagan was seventeen years old in people years when she crossed over that beautiful Rainbow Bridge. That is 119 years old in dog years.

She was completely deaf and had lost much of her eyesight. For the most part, she had come to rely mainly on her sense of smell.

She also relied heavily on little Mousie too. Mousie, our other Yorkie, helped Meagan get around the house. Mousie let Meagan know when it was time to get up. She also let her know when it was time to eat or when it was time to bark to alert us when someone rang the doorbell.

Meagan came into my life when she was about a year and half old. She was traveling with her breeder who happened to be showing dogs at a national dog show in Raleigh, North Carolina. Meagan was not in the show. She was in the breeder's hotel room with a few other dogs who were deemed not quite up to par for the show ring.

The breeder told me that she had three young dogs for sale. I decided to go and take a look. Inside the hotel room there was a baby crib filled with puppies. The woman took out each of the three puppies she had for sale. She carefully placed them on the floor. The first puppy was really cute and extremely friendly. I sat on the floor and she immediately climbed up in my lap and licked my face.

I watched the second puppy running around, playing with a little toy.

Then there was Meagan, who just stood staring at me as if she were wishing I would leave. Meagan was bigger and older than the other two puppies.

"What's wrong with that dog?" I asked the breeder, pointing to Meagan.

"Oh, she's a pretty one," the breeder replied. "But as you can see, she has a little bit of an attitude."

Considering that a challenge, I decided to pick her up and pet her. She ran from me, through an open door and into the bathroom. I followed her and knelt down beside her. Meagan made her way around the backside of the toilet and hid everything but her head. She kept that out in clear view with her eyes fixed directly on me.

She obviously knew she was trapped. I reached behind the fixture and picked her up. I petted her and placed her next to the other two puppies on the floor. The first puppy came right back to me again and Meagan ran up under the crib to hide.

"I guess I know which you want," the breeder laughed.

"Yes. I have definitely made up my mind. I want that one," I said, pointing to Meagan.

"Are you sure?"

"Yes, I am sure. I think she may be the one that needs me the most."

I brought Meagan home to live with me. It took a few weeks for her to learn to trust me, but eventually she did. In fact, I soon became her very best friend and she became the queen of the house. She traveled with me everywhere. She even flew on airplanes in her own little carrier with her name embroidered on it.

Meagan had quite a life, but age finally caught up with her.

The house is much quieter now without Meagan. We miss her bark in the morning and I still look for her in her little bed whenever I walk past the laundry room.

It is my sincere hope that the contribution that was made in honor of Meagan's life will help another animal find their way into a loving home. I know that there are many homeless animals ready and waiting to give someone else the opportunity to experience the unconditional love and joy that Meagan brought into our lives.

Max

Mike and I spent some time working out in the backyard, trying to clean up a mountain of unwanted leaves. Several times throughout the day, the lawn mower would sputter, choke, and then let out a loud backfire. Whenever that would happen, I would instinctively look around and yell, "Where's Max?" Then, I would drop the rake in my hand and head to see where he had run to hide.

Max is our ten-year-old Golden Retriever and he is deathly afraid of all loud noises. The rocking chair on the front porch is Max's favorite place to hide beneath. Each time I find Max beneath the rocking chair, his eyes are closed tightly as though he thinks what he is unable to see won't hurt him.

His second favorite place to hide is in my neighbor's garage, preferably in the backseat of their car, if the window happens to be down. Thunder, fireworks, the backfiring vehicles, nail guns, and especially loud booms associated with the military exercises at Fort Bragg are enough to cause Max to become unglued and search for a place to hide.

Before Max came into my life, I always considered Golden Retrievers to be fearless hunting dogs. I was surprised when I discovered a large, strong animal could actually become completely unnerved by an occasional clap of thunder. Our Max is no hunting dog. The sound of a gunshot would be enough to send him running helter-skelter to a neighboring county.

In fact, the fear of loud noises is probably what landed him in the dog pound where I discovered him about eight years ago. Max was on the adoption side of the Cumberland County animal shelter. He was alone in a small pen. The attendant in charge of feeding the animals and cleaning the pens actually pointed Max out to me.

"I think that is a really nice dog. I don't know why he hasn't been adopted," he told me.

According to the shelter's director, Max had been waiting for a home so long that he was scheduled to be euthanized in the next few days if no one came in to adopt him. All they could tell me about Max was that they believed he must have been on the road for quite some time, just trying to survive.

No one really even knew Max was a Golden Retriever. He was listed on the chart in the shelter as a mixed breed. Extremely thin and frail, he only weighed fifty-two pounds. His fur was dry and bleached from the sun and malnutrition, and he really didn't look much like the any kind of special breed at all.

I remember stepping inside Max's pen that day to get a closer look at him.

Max came over to get a closer look at me too.

Then he suddenly turned, sat down on my foot, and leaned his entire body against my leg.

This dog knows what he is doing, I thought to myself.

It was at that very moment I made the decision to adopt Max and bring him home to live with me. After a vet check, we learned Max was extremely underweight for his size and breed and he had the early stages of heartworm disease. We immediately started him on treatment for the heartworms.

Max soon learned that he would get regular meals, treats, and all he wanted to eat living in his new home. He blossomed into an absolutely beautiful and loyal companion.

It is hard to believe that eight years has passed since Max came home with me from the animal shelter. He now weighs in close to one hundred pounds. He has a thick, bright orange coat and he is a kind, gentle, and happy dog. He continues to remain a little insecure, however.

When he gets a treat, he wants his head patted to say it is okay before he goes to indulge.

And he is really, really scared of loud noises.

Eight years later, Max still sits on my foot and leans his entire body against my leg, just like he did that first day at the animal shelter. So it obviously wasn't simply a cute trick played by a sly dog wanting to find a way to escape a pending death penalty that fateful day I visited the shelter. It is just the way ole Max is, and I wouldn't trade him for the world.

There are many dogs just like Max at the local animal shelter who are in desperate need of a good home. There are some beautiful cats, too. Just like Max, they are all sitting patiently waiting for someone with a warm heart and a loving home to come in, discover them, and adopt them, before it is too late.

Unsung Heroes for Animals

A few months ago, a dog arrived at the local animal shelter, starved and on the verge of death. The small German shorthaired pointer was emaciated to the point you could easily count each one of her ribs. She weighed in at twenty-three pounds, less than half the weight of a healthy dog of her breed and size.

Her back legs were covered with raw, bloody abrasions.

Shelter attendants nursed the dog, who was understandably shy and a little fearful of people. When her allowed time at the facility was up, the shelter reached out to see if a rescue group could possibly help.

After seeing her picture, I contacted my sister-in-law, Ann. She has German shorthaired pointers and is also connected to a rescue organization for the breed. I sent her pictures of the starved dog, and asked if there was any way she could get her some help.

Ann contacted a rescue organization.

Shortly after, arrangements got underway and that is when this little dog's amazing journey began. First, the dog was transported to Raleigh, North Carolina by a county animal shelter volunteer. The volunteer met Ann, who in turn, transported the dog to another town to be examined by a veterinarian that works closely with the rescue group.

It was at this point the little dog was also given her name, Faye.

The vet noted Faye's starving and weakened condition and administered treatment which was paid for by the rescue organization. The following day, the vet deemed Faye healthy enough to make the important third leg of her journey, the one that would take her to a new foster family.

With all the rescue organization's foster homes filled to capacity in North Carolina, Faye was to be taken to neighboring Tennessee for foster care. Faye left the vet's office with yet another volunteer from the rescue group.

Then, in a manner very much resembling a relay race, the little dog was driven the miles of stretches down roads and highways, delivered from one volunteer to another, all the way to her foster family in Tennessee.

A total of ten volunteer drivers each took a turn in helping Faye along her journey. Faye would remain safe in her foster home to be nursed back to health, socialized, and loved until a permanent home could be found for her.

It has been three months since little Faye left the animal shelter. I have been trying to keep up with her journey via the internet. Last week, I received the news that Faye has been officially adopted and living in her forever home.

I was sent pictures. The transformation of this once shy, starving little dog is nothing short of remarkable.

No one person or volunteer brought about this positive outcome for Faye. Working together as a team, many volunteers did their small part to help. It was the collective efforts of many that created a "fairy-tail" ending for a deserving little dog. That is why I wanted to share Faye's story. There are many unsung heroes that work tirelessly behind the scenes for shelter animals like Faye. These include shelter attendants, shelter volunteers, rescue organizations and their volunteers, veterinarians who support these groups, and those willing to open their homes to provide foster care for animals in need. Often this work is done quietly with little or no recognition.

Their reward is simply in knowing they have helped a helpless animal.

Epilogue

Faye's story is the exception and not the rule. Unfortunately, most shelter pets do not experience a happy ending like Faye. However, with more shelter and rescue volunteers willing to do a small part, the chances increase that more animals like Faye will end up in a loving home.

Cats Are No Dogs

A neighbor friend of mine joked with me one day that he thought I was showing partiality to the dogs. He was making reference to the pictures I send in each week to be featured in the newspaper as shelter pets needing adoption for this paper. He said he had observed more pictures of dogs than cats.

You see, my friend is a cat person. Although he doesn't actually own one, he and his wife do have a special grand cat that goes by the name of "The Professor." He sends me pictures of the Professor from time to time.

Now I love cats just as much as I love dogs, so my friend's comment got me thinking. As a result, I asked permission to feature two shelter pets in the paper each week—one dog and one cat. This means one more animal that can potentially find a forever home. It also demonstrates a total fairness to both the canine and feline populations. It definitely serves to make my excursions to the animal shelter more of an adventure.

Most of us who have been around cats and dogs understand that there are distinct differences between the two species. One of the most noted is that dogs want to please people. Cats expect people to please them.

Getting a decent picture of the shelter dog each week is usually a breeze. After selecting the dog, I simply dangle a treat in the air in front of the dog with one hand and snap a picture with my camera using my other hand. The dog usually looks straight at the camera like it knows exactly what I am trying to do. Sometimes I don't even have to hold up the treat. The dog just poses for me. That is because dogs seek approval and for the most part, they cooperate.

Cats, on the other hand, are a completely different story. Selecting the shelter cat each week is the easiest part of the entire process. Getting a decent picture of the cat, one that can be published, is far more complex. For example, if I hold a treat in the air in front of a cat, I am usually met with a look of total disgust. Displaying a cat toy might gain attention for a few moments, but that is only if the cat is working to gain control of it, making for a very fuzzy picture. When the cat finally figures out I want it to look at my camera, well then it usually looks the other direction.

My trip to the shelter last week is a prime example of the difference between dogs and cats. I entered the dog adoption area, grabbed a few dog biscuits from a plastic bucket, and then picked out a cute adult shepherd mix named Jasper for the picture. After spending a few minutes with him, I held a treat in the air and Jasper looked directly at my camera. Three clicks and I had a decent picture.

I gave ole Jasper a treat and a pat on the head and then proceeded to the cat room. There, I decided to take a picture of Jose, a beautiful Siamese mix. I slowly opened the cage door and Jose immediately looked at me with some suspicion. I leaned inside the cage to pet him, which he graciously allowed. After a few moments, I actually caught myself asking Jose for permission to take his picture. Jose rolled over on his back to check me out from a different angle. I petted him again, nudged him just a little, and tried to get him to stand upright for his picture. Of course, he didn't. He just continued to lie there, upside down, staring at me.

I leaned into the cage again to see if I could perhaps lift him and turn him right side up for the picture. That is when I felt something yanking my hair. It was the yellow kitten in the cage just above Jose's. The feisty little kitty had both of his front legs fully extended between the bars of his cage and had somehow managed to reach down far enough to grab hold of my hair.

He must have been quite proud of his accomplishment because he was pulling hard and apparently had no intentions of letting go. I reached up with one hand to try to detangle my hair from the kitten's claws while at same time watching to make sure Jose, who appeared somewhat amused, remained secure in his cage.

With the yellow kitten's claws still wrapped up in my hair, I felt another tug suddenly pulling down around my neck. It was the gray tabby cat in the pen just below Jose. This crafty little fellow had reached his front legs out far enough to grab hold of my camera strap and was pulling it with all his might.

At this point, as I worked to detangled myself from all four little cat paws, I could not help but think about my friend. However, I managed to get it back together and to finally get Jose standing upright for his picture.

It took a mere twenty-six clicks of the camera to get Jose to finally look at me. And then I think I just got lucky.

Weasel

Having a great personality will take you far in life, even if you are a barn cat from humble beginnings. Take Weasel, for example. Weasel recently gained celebrity status when her easygoing disposition was captured in a picture that won the WRAL television pet photo contest. In the winning photo, Weasel is seen posing with her best friend, Butter Bean the horse.

Weasel had a rather rough start in life. I am thinking that may have contributed to her ability to take everything in stride. She was born beneath a trailer and orphaned as a very young kitten. She survived on leftover pieces of dry dog food she found in a dish belonging to an old bulldog named Mike.

For whatever reason, that old bulldog befriended Weasel and allowed her to share his food. He also allowed her to crawl in his doghouse at night and sleep with him in order to stay warm. I guess that may have been the beginnings of Weasel's understanding that you will get a lot farther in life if you learn to get along with everyone, including old bulldogs. After all, it can sometimes be a dog-eat-dog, or cat, world.

When I heard about this tenacious little kitty and her will to survive, I decided to bring her home with me and make her our barn cat. A trip to the vet found her to be in surprisingly good health and she immediately took to barn life. When she was a kitten, Weasel would entertain herself by hiding in the hay. You never knew where she was or when she would "pop" out and try to scare you. Each time that would happen, I would laugh and say, "Pop goes the weasel!" That is how Weasel got her name.

Weasel knows both the barn and the surrounding pasture like the back of her paw. She loves the outdoors and spends her days keeping watch over the barn and chasing butterflies through the pasture. She easily makes friends with everyone she meets.

She peacefully coexists with chickens.

But most of all, she enjoys hanging out with her best friend Butter Bean. The two have developed a special bond and they are inseparable. Weasel works hard to keep the mice out of Butter Bean's food. And in turn, Weasel finds safety and warmth sleeping high on Butter Bean's back.

I'll Take Slim Pick

We have a small fishpond in our yard that, up until recently, only served as home to water bugs, tadpoles, and an occasional bullfrog. We drained the little pond a few weeks ago and repaired the fountain that circulates the water. The bottom of the pond was cleared of leaves and debris and then the water was refilled.

After the pond was ready, I made a trip to the pet store hoping to purchase some koi fish. Koi, also known as Japanese carp, are ornamental fish that are commonly kept in outdoor fishponds.

The first pet store where I stopped did not have any koi fish. I left that store and drove to another. When I walked through the door of the second store, a young man greeted me with a large smile. "Can I help you?" he asked.

"Do you have any koi fish?"

The young man pointed toward the back of the store. "We do, but we only have slim pickins right now," he said.

In the fish section, he showed me the tank marked "koi fish." I saw one scrawny little white fish swimming around in the tank.

"Is that Slim Pickins?"

"Yes," he said, a little embarrassed. "He's kind of puny. I guess no one wanted him." I stared at the skinny little fish for a minute as he swam around in circles, alone in the tank. "I think I'll take Slim Pickins," I said to his amazement.

Without hesitation, he quickly picked up a net, scooped up the fish, and dumped him into a plastic bag of water. He blew air into the bag and tied it with a rubber band. After paying at the checkout counter, I headed straight home with Slim Pickins. The directions said to float the inflated bag for approximately thirty minutes in order to acclimate the fish to the water temperature in the new environment. After floating the bag for the required amount of time, I released Slim Pickins into his new watery home. He was so small I wasn't sure he would survive.

At first the little white fish appeared to explore the bottom of the pond. Then after a few minutes, he suddenly disappeared beneath a rock. For several weeks, I looked but didn't see Slim Pickins anywhere in the pond. This past weekend, I was at still another pet store purchasing food for Mildred our parrot. In the fish section, I noticed there were not many fish in the koi tank.

When an employee came to help me, I was amazed to hear him tell me the same thing I had heard at the previous store.

"If you want koi fish," he said, "we only have Slim Pickins today."

"You can't possibly have Slim Pickins because I bought him three weeks ago," I mused. After I explained, he laughed. I did tell him that I thought Slim Pickins might like to have a few friends.

I left this pet store with three more koi fish—Buckshot, Lady, and Earnhart.

Buckshot is white with small round orange dots all over his body.

Lady is bright orange with beautiful flowing fins that look like eloquent scarves.

And Earnhart, well he is really fast.

After floating the three plastic bags for thirty minutes, I released them one by one in the water. That is when Slim Pickins suddenly appeared. Over the past few weeks, the scrawny little fish had grown three times his previous size. He immediately joined the other fish and swam with them. Slim Pickins had survived by hiding and now appeared to find comfort in having Buckshot, Lady, and Earnhart join him in the pond.

I think fish are smart.

Perhaps that is why they prefer to be in schools.

Butter Bean

The other day, Mike called me on my cell phone.

"Where are you?" he asked, sounding a little out of breath.

I told him I was in Walmart.

"Where are you?"

"I am just now leaving the barn," he replied. "I had to go catch Butter Bean. She's been running all over the neighborhood!"

Butter Bean is our horse. Evidently, the pasture gate was not properly secured that morning and she must have figured out how to get it open. Butter Bean had been spotted grazing her way through the neighbor's yards, making her way up the road, having herself a good ole time. Mike had been called at work by a concerned neighbor who had witnessed her escape.

When Butter Bean saw Mike's truck going down the gravel road toward the barn, he said that she turned and galloped back as fast as she could. I guess she was probably thinking it must be time to eat. Eating, by the way, is what Butter Bean does best.

I could tell by Mike's voice he was relieved that Butter Bean wasn't hurt, and that she was safely back in the pasture where she belongs. Butter Bean and Mike are good friends, even though I have to admit they did get off to a rather rocky start.

It all happened a few years after we were married when we decided to get a horse.

Although I had always wanted one, I never had a horse of my own, and I really didn't know very much about them. Mike, on the other hand, has been around horses most of his life. After searching for weeks, we finally found Butter Bean at Jerry and Liz King's ranch located in a nearby community. I thought she was the most beautiful horse I had ever seen and I fell in love with her the moment I saw her.

Liz, who is an excellent rider herself, basically assured us that Butter Bean was childproof. She was gentle, solid, and would make a really good horse for a beginning rider like myself.

We made arrangements to get Butter Bean transported to our pasture and decided it would be best to let her become familiar with her new surroundings for a couple of weeks. I would visit with her daily and spend hours brushing her, walking her, and just getting to know her. Then, very early one cool Saturday morning, Mike woke up and announced that this would be a perfect day to ride Butter Bean.

We drove to the barn at the break of day and got out the old saddle and equipment he still had from his former horse, Star. I brushed Butter Bean down and my husband placed the new blanket I had bought her and the old saddle up on the horse's back.

He cinched it up tightly.

"Isn't that too tight?" I asked.

"It's got to be tight," he said. "You don't want it to fall off the horse, do you?"

Then he cinched the saddle up once again, even tighter.

This time Butter Bean got a funny look in her eye, but I figured he knew what he was doing.

Next, Mike held the reins and instructed me to climb up on the horse.

Now I have to admit I was extremely nervous, but I did get on. I could tell from the way Butter Bean was acting that she wasn't very happy about it. She was dancing around a little with her front feet. I told my husband I wanted to get off.

"Don't be silly," he said. "She is just fine."

Then I noticed Butter Bean's ears. They were flat back on her head.

"I'm getting off this horse and I'm getting off now!" I said.

Seeing the panicked look on my face, Mike helped me get down off the horse.

"Let me show you how to do this," Mike said, grabbing the reins and climbing onto the horse.

I could only lean back against the fence with my mouth open wide when Butter Bean obviously decided enough was enough. I have watched plenty of rodeo shows on television. However, I will readily admit I have never seen a horse that even came close to the moves old Butter Bean performed that morning with my husband on her back.

She jumped straight up, all four feet leaving the ground at once, and spun 360 degrees in midair.

When her feet hit the ground, she arched her back and bucked sideways one good time at what appeared to me to be a forty-five-degree angle. Mike sailed about ten feet through the air like a major league fastball.

And that was pretty much it.

On the way to the hospital, Mike was stretched out somehow halfway between the front and backseat of the car. Waiting to be seen in the emergency room, I overheard the doctor talking to the nurse coming down the hall.

"So which room do they have John Wayne in?" he asked.

Fortunately for us, Mike left the hospital that day with only some minor scratches, a cracked rib, and a bruised ego. So what made Butter Bean, our gentle childproof horse, turn into a rodeo star that chilly fall morning? Turns out the girth on the old saddle we were using was dried and brittle. When the saddle was cinched, it was pinching Butter Bean's stomach and pulling her hair. Apparently the harder it was cinched, the more it pinched.

Butter Bean remains a wonderful and gentle horse.

She lives the good life at the barn.

By the way, I did get a new saddle for Christmas that year.

Of course, Mike had to take a little ribbing, pardon the pun, about being thrown to the ground by a horse named Butter Bean. He asked me if we could rename her Killer Bee but I refused.

He also claims he stayed on for seven seconds that day. I tell him he probably did, but to tell you the truth, I really think it was more like two.

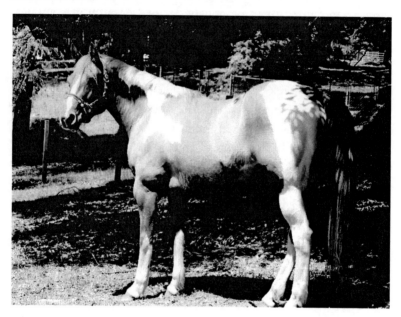

Junior Jr.

As I kid, I spent many a Sunday afternoon hanging around my grandmother Carter's chicken coop in Massey Hill. The wooden coop was located inside a fenced area in my grandmother's backyard. At that time, Massey Hill had not been annexed into the city of Fayetteville, so raising chickens there was a fairly common practice.

Mostly, I liked to watch the chickens as they scratched around in the dirt. Sometimes, I would sneak inside the coop and play with the plastic Easter eggs my grandmother would place in their nests in order to trick the hens into laying. Although I enjoyed watching them, I never really thought that any of those chickens were all that intelligent.

In fact, if someone had told me back then that a chicken could actually have a personality, I probably would not have believed them. How could a chicken, with a brain smaller than the size of a pea, be intelligent or have a personality?

Of course, that is before I got to know a little bantam rooster by the name of Junior Jr. Junior Jr. is my pet rooster and he lives down at our barn located just outside the Hope Mills town limits.

The first thing people usually want to know is how Junior Jr. got his name.

He was named after his father, Junior.

His mother, Little Bit, was a tiny black hen about the size of one's fist.

Junior Jr. hatched out in the spring of 2006, around Mother's Day. When he was just a biddy, he spent most of his day in the woods. I always worried about whether he would find his way back to the barn in the evening to roost or be eaten by some wild hungry creature. But Junior Jr. always managed to make his way back to the barn. Little Bit, his mother, wasn't so lucky. So Junior Jr. grew up around a horse and barn cats.

Now Junior Jr. thinks he is a cat.

He loves to eat cat food.

He is the first to make it to the cat treats when they are placed on the steps of the barn.

He loves to have his head scratched.

He sits in my lap in the rocking chair and he comes running when I call "Here Kitty, Kitty."

Junior Jr. is well known by those living in the neighborhood. His crowing helps them keep track of the time. He welcomes the sunrise each morning with a loud crow and lets everyone know when the sun is getting ready to go down in the evening. And according to one neighbor, he occasionally gets mixed up and lets everyone know when it is three or four o'clock in the afternoon too.

When he is out and about, Junior Jr. mostly scratches around the barnyard for bugs and worms. In the heat of the day, however, he finds shade beneath the barn hanging around with the cats.

And at night, he finds safety in a bird cage located on the porch of the barn. I guess for a rooster, one could say Junior Jr. truly lives the good life. He dines each day on an endless supply of cracked corn. But more than anything, he looks forward to Sundays. That's the day he gets a leftover biscuit from the Cracker Barrel.

My grandmother Carter loved her chickens. I guess I must take after my grandmother.

Banana Rat

We have a small fishpond in our yard that has been empty of both water and fish for almost two years. At least that is what we thought until the other day when we were surprised to discover a little six-inch koi fish hiding beneath the leaves and muck in a small hole located at the bottom of the pond.

The hole, where the pond's pump is housed, is only about a foot square in size. It stays filled with the rainwater and the leaves which collect in it from time to time. My husband discovered the white and gold fish the other day when he went to pull the pump from the hole.

We drained the pond during the summer of 2010 shortly after all the fish, we thought, were tragically devoured by a large heron that showed up one day for a quick and easy snack. So from our estimation the poor little forgotten fish must have been in that small dark hole, hiding beneath the pump for almost two years. How this fish managed to survive is beyond me.

Anyway, my thoughts were that any fish that wanted to live that badly deserves a chance in life. So I went to the store and purchased an aquarium.

After setting it up, we captured the fish and placed her in the new tank, complete with gravel, rocks, and two plastic plants.

The first day, the little fish seemed shy and skittish. We figured it was probably the first time she had been able to see anything and was probably scared to death.

However, by the second day, she began to adjust to her new environment and was swimming around in happy little circles.

The fish needed a name so we thought it would be fun to ask Mildred, our parrot, what we should call her. Since you never know what Mildred is going to say, we knew it was luck of the draw but agreed that whatever she said first would be the fish's new name.

Mildred has her favorite words. She used two of them when asked her opinion about what we should call the Koi.

And that is how our new fish, Banana Rat, got her name.

Part V

On Work and Technology

BELLS AND WHISTLES

Tweeting Away on Twitter

Twitter is an online social networking technology that is quickly growing in popularity. Several of my friends use Twitter and although some encouraged me to do so, I always thought Twitter was one form of communication that would come and go without me. With e-mail, snail mail, landlines, cell phones, and all the meetings I attend, the last thing I thought I needed in my life was another source of communication. When someone asked me if I was a tweeter, my standard line was "Tweeting is for the birds."

This weekend, however, after reading a news article, my curiosity finally got the best of me. I decided to sign up for Twitter. At first, I wasn't sure if what I was doing was called twittering or tweeting. There is a short instructional video you can watch online at Twitter.com, but like everything else, checking the instructions is what I do only when all else fails. However, I did finally figure out that what I was doing is called "tweeting" on Twitter.

After you sign up for Twitter, the program will automatically search your computer's electronic address book and identify all of your friends and contacts that are also signed up to use Twitter. Then, it will ask you which of those friends and contacts you would like to "follow."

Following someone simply means that you can view all the tweets that particular person writes. A "tweet" is a short typed message, no longer than 140 characters in length. You can request to follow tweets made by your friends, family members, colleagues, reporters, even Hollywood celebrities.

Others can choose to follow you and read your tweets.

You can tweet to let people know where you are, what you are doing, what you think, how you feel, or what is happening around you. Keeping your tweet to 140 or less characters is the trick, and can prove a bit difficult for long-winded folks like me.

You can read and send tweets from your cell phone or from your computer. Tweeting is similar to sending a text message from your phone or an instant message from your computer. After you tweet, your message can be viewed instantly by everyone who follows you on Twitter. Of course, if you don't want someone following you for some reason, you can always block them from reading your tweets.

So far, I have "tweeted" twice.

You can also use Twitter to get breaking news in the form of tweets before it is published in the paper or online, especially if you choose to follow a reporter or a news source. For example, the first "news tweet" I read after signing onto Twitter concerned a rumor about a nest of three hundred water moccasins in Hope Mills Lake.

Now that tweet got my attention. I left Twitter and my tweeting to go out and look for the three hundred water moccasins.

Fortunately, I did not see any.

Hopefully it was just a tweeted rumor.

So far, I have two followers signed up to read my "tweets" and I am following twelve people. Although I am new to the technology, Twitter has actually been around since 2006. In a world of instant communication, what will future technology allow us to do?

With all this Twitter and tweeting, it does makes one wonder twat's next.

Viva Las Vegas

Last week, I went to work where most people go to play, Las Vegas, Nevada. To me, Vegas is one of those "nice to visit but wouldn't want to live there" kind of places.

I don't really get into all the shows.

I am also not much of a gambler.

I think the biggest gamble I ever took in Vegas was getting married there. And no, Elvis didn't perform the wedding ceremony.

I guess there is something about gambling that kind of goes against my basic philosophy about money and machines. I believe that if you put your hard-earned money into a machine, you should expect to get something in return, like a gumball, a candy bar, or a Coke.

In Vegas, I observed lots of people putting their hard-earned money into machines and never getting anything in return.

Something about that just doesn't sit right with me.

During my visit, however, everyone kept asking me if I had played any of the machines and won any money. They looked at me kind of funny when I told them I hadn't gambled at all. I actually had someone tell me I needed to lighten up a little and take a risk. After all, I was in Las Vegas!

So I buckled under the pressure and decided I would give it a try.

I set my gambling limit at $10 and told myself once it was gone, it was gone.

The only two casino games I really understand how to play are blackjack and the slot machine, also known as the one-arm bandit for a pretty good reason. Looking around for a game to play, I noticed a special room in the casino with a sign over the entrance.

According to the sign, the room was designated for high stakes gamblers only. Curiosity got the best of me, so I peeked inside.

There weren't a lot of people in the room and there didn't appear to be much going on. I assumed I wouldn't qualify to enter anyway with my $10 limit. So I kept on walking until I eventually found the blackjack tables.

There were large crowds gathered around the tables and lots of money changing hands. No one was smiling. Everyone had really serious looks on their faces and they weren't talking to each other. It didn't look like they were having much fun to me.

So I decided to bypass blackjack and look for a slot machine where you didn't have to play with other people. It took me a while, but I finally discovered the fruit machines. Those are the slot machines that have the pictures of cherries and lemons on them that spin around. I climbed up on a stool and checked out the machine before inserting my money.

According to the directions, you could wage a bet for only a nickel.

Now that appealed to me.

I knew I could get more tries for my money and could play longer that way. Judging by the pictures on the machine, you would win credits if your spin resulted in a complete row of fruit or a row of bars. There were a few other combinations that would also score you credits, and a symbol representing a wild card that could count toward anything.

It sounded simple enough to me.

I inserted $5 into the slot on the machine and began to play. After a while, I actually started winning. In fact, at one point, I was up by thirty credits. That was when I considered cashing in, but then I realized that it would only be $1.50. So I decided to wait until I could get a little further ahead and win a little more money before hitting the cashier stand.

I kept putting in nickels until I had to quit. According to the machine, the game was over. I got up from my stool with the final score being fruit machine $5, and me nothing.

With my remaining $5, I searched the casino for the video poker machines.

It took me a while but I finally found them. The video poker machine had higher stakes than the fruit machine. You had to bet a quarter each turn. Hoping that lady luck would be on my side this time, I inserted my remaining $5 into the machine.

Before I knew it, the game was over.

The final score was video poker machine $5, and me nothing.

Before going to the airport that evening, I decided to spend my remaining hours in Las Vegas shopping. Now that is something I really do enjoy. The best part was that when they put my money into the cash register machine, I actually got a T-shirt and two hats in return.

Juicing It Up

One sleepless night, I was aimlessly flipping through the TV channels when I came across an infomercial for a juicer. According to the spokesperson, the kitchen gadget was designed to convert whole fruits and vegetables into juice without mess or fuss. He said that juicing promotes a healthy lifestyle.

Up to this point, the only juicer I was familiar with was my mom's which I guess would now be considered an antique. It amounted to a little more than a small glass dish with a grooved dome protruding in the center. It required the manual twisting and grinding of half an orange or a lemon in order to extract a small bit of juice.

Then you had to fish seeds out of the dish.

So I decided to watch the thirty-minute demonstration and the sales pitch for the product.

The juicer spokesperson dropped a whole apple, stem, seeds and all, into the machine. He flipped a switch and the apple traveled down a metal shoot. Apple juice began to stream into a small container located on the side of the machine.

He did the same with a carrot, without even peeling it.

Bright orange carrot juice spewed into the container.

Then he juiced celery stalks, tomatoes, and a cucumber, all the while touting the health benefits gained from juicing.

I was hooked.

So the next day, I did some research and went and purchased a juicer.

I set up the appliance on my kitchen counter next to the coffeepot.

I was reading the "Quick Start" guide when Mike noticed the new machine sitting on the counter.

The following conversation ensued.

"What is that?" he asked.

"It's a juicer," I replied.

"What does this mean?" he asked.

"It means we are going to make our own juice."

"Does this mean we are on the juice?" His question was followed by a slight pause.

"It means we are going to be making our own juice."

"Does this mean we are not going to be eating real food anymore?"

I was silent at this point. I knew where the conversation was headed.

Obviously my husband must have been listening to the infomercial when I thought he was sleeping. The fellow on the infomercial had stated facts about the benefits of juicing, which includes a change of lifestyle.

Mike looked intently at the juicer.

"Can you put a pork chop in that thing?" he asked.

For breakfast the next day, Mike had a glass of freshly made tomato, cucumber, and celery juice. He drank it while eating his sausage, grits, and biscuits. He even said it was pretty good.

I guess sometimes slow change is better than no change.

The Coffeepot

Our old "Mr. Coffee" pot finally wore out and we have a new coffeemaker in our home. This time we upgraded. The old coffeemaker had one switch—on and off. This new one comes equipped with a few more bells and whistles, or as my dad would say, more things on it to break.

Our new coffeemaker is made of stainless steel and comes with a thermal carafe designed to keep the coffee hot and fresh for hours. Another neat feature on this new machine is that it beeps to let you know when your coffee is ready. A series of three faint beeps signals you that the coffee has finished brewing.

Mildred, our parrot, has already mastered the sound and has figured out how to send us running prematurely to the pot each morning.

Our new coffeemaker comes with a digital clock that glows a bright blue color in the dark. It has a preset function that allows you to prepare everything in the evening and have your coffee waiting for you first thing in the morning. In our house, that is really important. That first cup of coffee is what seems to set everything into motion for the day. To me, there is nothing more pleasant than to wake up in the morning to the smell of freshly brewed coffee.

Although this new coffeemaker seems to brew a little bit faster than our last one, the jury is still out as to whether the coffee tastes as good.

Coffee has always been a big part of my life. Growing up, the coffeepot in our house was on both day and night. People would drop by to visit and the first thing they were offered was a cup of hot coffee. Local police officers would take a break from their duties and stop by our house for a cup of my mom's coffee. The mail carrier would be offered a cup of coffee on cold winter days. He would stand on the front porch for a few minutes, resting and warming up with a cup of the hot beverage.

Our house was so well known for its coffee, someone gave my mom a plaque that read "Ask about Our Free Cup of Coffee." She hung it proudly by the coffeepot in the kitchen.

Back then, the coffee of choice at our house was Eight O'Clock brand coffee. It came in a red bag with black letters from the local A&P grocery store. The man at the A&P would grind the beans as I stood close by, watching and smelling. I actually thought Eight O'Clock coffee was the only kind of coffee there was until I grew up and discovered there were others.

Of course, as kids, we would ask about drinking coffee because the grown-ups seemed to enjoy it so much. We always got the same answer—no, because it would stunt our growth. I was pretty short anyway, so that answer was good enough for me.

Then I went to college and things changed.

College exams caused us to pull what we referred to as "all-nighters." These were nights we stayed awake as long as we could, studying before an important test the next day. Some of these all-nighters took us well into the wee hours of the morning. More often than not, they were held at the Shoney's Restaurant in Greenville, North Carolina. There you could sit in a safe environment and drink coffee with free unlimited refills. The coffee seemed to help us stay awake while we studied for our exams.

I guess that is where I officially began drinking coffee.

Fast forward three decades. I am not sure whether it stunted my growth, but I am still about the same height I was in college. The coffeepot in our house now remains on both day and night. Starbucks is my favorite brand of coffee, although we only buy it occasionally as a special treat. And when someone comes to our house for a visit, they know the first thing they will be offered is a hot cup of coffee. That is why I am hoping this fancy new stainless steel coffeemaker of ours will withstand the test of use and time.

Meanwhile, I will look forward to waking up each morning and smelling the coffee.

The Hummer

I guess you could say that I have always been a little directionally challenged. Even something as simple as finding my way around a shopping mall can be a little difficult for me. So you can only imagine the nightmare I experience when I have to drive in unfamiliar cities and towns.

But that is exactly what my job often requires me to do.

That is why I was delighted this summer when I was introduced to the Global Positioning System. A GPS device came standard with my rental car at the Richmond Airport.

At first, I wasn't sure I could operate it because I am also a little technologically challenged. But the system was labeled "Never Lost" and that idea appealed to me enough to want to give it a try. It really wasn't all that difficult. After pushing a few buttons, the machine actually walked me through the process step by step. At the airport, I programmed in the street address of the hotel where I would be staying in Williamsburg.

When I started to drive the car, a lady's calm voice came through the speakers of the system. The lady told me when to turn left, when to turn right, and even when to continue on straight.

On the highway, she directed me to the off-ramps and a bell sounded when I was to exit. In fact, after a while, I stopped paying attention to the road signs and just listened to the GPS lady as she gave me directions. A couple of times, I even caught myself talking to her like an old friend.

The trip ended at the hotel parking lot entrance as she announced a pleasant "You have arrived!" This first experience with the "Never Lost" system had me hooked.

I told myself that I would never again rent a car without one.

So last week, when I had to make the drive between the St. Louis Airport and Springfield Illinois, I explicitly stated that I required a car with a "Never Lost" machine when making my reservation.

The person taking the reservation laughed and said, "You and everyone else."

When I arrived in St. Louis, it was late in the evening. I went directly to the rental car desk because my name was not listed on the board designating which car on the lot was mine. The fellow behind the desk said, "Ma'am, your name was not listed because we are out of vehicles with a 'Never Lost' system."

"You can't be!" I complained. "I specifically asked for one when I made my reservation." Then I added, in the best shaky voice I could muster, "Sir, I don't know where I am going and it is really dark."

Seeing the panicked look on my face, the gentleman picked up the phone and made a call. After a brief conversation, he turned to me and said, "Ma'am, we do have one car at this facility with a 'Never Lost' device."

"I'll take it!" I said.

"But I am not sure you want to drive it," he grinned.

I quickly replied, "If it has a 'Never Lost,' I definitely want to drive it".

"Fine," he mused. "You just rented yourself a Hummer."

"A Hummer? Isn't that one of those huge vehicles that looks like an army tank?"

"Yes, ma'am. It's a great big tank with a 'Never Lost' system," he chuckled.

I have to admit that driving a Hummer down the highway at 70 mph was an interesting experience. At first, I was intimidated by its size. Then I suddenly felt a rush of power as I watched all the other cars slow down and move slightly to the side of the road as the Hummer and I made our way down the interstate.

And the nice lady with the calm voice once again talked to me the entire trip.

She helped direct me all the way to the Crown Plaza Hotel in Springfield, Illinois. Later, I told a friend about my adventure humming down the highway in the Hummer. He couldn't stop laughing.

Then he asked, "You didn't hit anything, did you?"

"Of course not," I replied.

But I will admit that in the daylight on the way back to the airport the next day, I noticed several dead deer lying on the side of the road.

Nah, I thought.

Wasn't me!

Cell Phones

My cell phone has been on the blink for the past few days. Until recently, I never realized how much I have grown to depend on it. I use my cell phone for a lot of things. I use it to check and send e-mails. I read the local and national news on my phone. I even use it to check the weather. My phone sometimes doubles as my camera or my camcorder. When I am traveling, my cell phone transforms into my trusty alarm clock. And yes, sometimes I even use it to make phone calls.

Remember back, not too awfully long ago, when telephones were just plain old telephones? They were attached to the wall by a cord. They were not portable. You talked on the phone wherever the phone happened to be located.

Growing up, our telephone was in the kitchen on the counter. I remember my mom sitting at the kitchen table talking on the telephone for what seemed like hours without ever moving from the same kitchen chair. She seemed to enjoy it, too.

You didn't go to the phone store to purchase these telephones. They were placed in your homes by the phone company. As a kid, I remember being told that if we misused them in any way or made prank calls on them, the operator would make a personal trip to our house to remove them. I believed that, too.

Most of these telephones came in one color—black. But I do recall the day we got our first phone that was a different color. It was a light powder blue. I thought it was the fanciest thing I had ever seen.

These regular old telephones came with a receiver that attached to the body of the phone by a coiled plastic cord. You held one end of the receiver to your ear to listen and the other end to your mouth to speak. The cord would sometimes become entangled and knotted from use. Whenever that would happen, you would have to hold the cord in the air and let the receiver dangle downward. The receiver would spiral and spin until it finally untangled and straightened itself back out.

There were no buttons to push on these telephones either. Instead, there was a rotary dial. You had to stick your finger in the hole on the dial that corresponded with the number you wanted. Then you would slide your finger around until you came to a silver piece of metal that served as a stop. You would remove your finger from the hole and the dial would click its way back to the same spot you started.

Sometimes, the dial would become sluggish and drag. That is when you would have to force it back the other direction with your finger. The sluggishness and dragging would sometimes result in the inadvertent dialing of a wrong number. We were told that this was caused from using the phone with sticky hands. Mama would clean the dial with rubbing alcohol.

Interestingly enough, back then our phone number actually started with letters instead of numbers. Our number began with the letters H and U. I guess the H and U stood for the numbers 4 and 8. We referred to the H and U part of the number as "Hudson." When giving your number to someone, you would say Hudson and then state the remaining five numbers.

Then new phones began to appear that ironically foreshadowed times to come.

The first time I ever saw a car phone was on an episode of Batman. Batman had a car phone in the Batmobile. He used it to call police commissioner Gordon or to call Alfred, the butler, back in the bat cave. Of course, Commissioner Gordon answered Batman's calls on a special red phone in his office.

There was also a phone in 007's car and who could forget Maxwell Smart's infamous shoe phone on the television series Get Smart? As kids, we would walk around with our shoes held to our ears and pretend to be on the phone. If someone could have a phone in their car or in their shoe, it made me wonder if there might ever come a day that I could make a phone call and actually see my friends while we talked?

I eventually got my first car phone. It came in a black bag and it was about the size of a shoe box. It plugged into the cigarette lighter and I locked it away in the trunk whenever I left the car. My cell phone is now my car phone. It is the size of a credit card and it plugs into nothing. All of our house phones are now conveniently portable. But often as not, you have to perform a major search for them before you can make a call. And just the other day, I was in my office when my television rang. I used my remote control to answer it. It was an incoming video call from some friends of mine in California. It was great to hear from them, and it was even better to see them while we talked.

I bet even Maxwell Smart would have been totally impressed.

Airport Maneuvers

Just when I thought I had figured it all out, they have changed the rules again. The recent threat of another terror attack in Britain has caused our nation's airports to scrutinize security systems and make more adjustments. Consequently, I find myself once again trying to figure out the best, most efficient way to make my way through airports in the least amount of time with the least amount of hassle.

My job requires me to fly on a regular basis, sometimes weekly, so I spend a lot of time in airports. I even met my husband in an airport. I consider maneuvering through airports as a kind of science. You can study the system and once you figure it out, it is relatively easy to do. But the problem is, the system keeps changing.

Before 9/11, getting through airport check-in lines, past security checkpoints, to the gate and on the plane was a piece of cake. I had developed an effective strategy based on my study of the system. There weren't all that many security measures in place then, which is really scary when you think about it. My strategy was to always arrive at the airport at the very last minute. That way, I didn't have to wait around wasting valuable time. I could go straight to the gate and get on the plane. I never checked luggage. Carrying my luggage with me on the plane saved a lot of time. My luggage would always arrive with me at my final destination and I could avoid the headache of waiting around in baggage claim.

I always carried a snack and a bottle of water in my luggage just in case I got hungry or thirsty because I never wanted to find myself at the mercy of a busy or inattentive flight attendant. All in all, my strategy really worked well for me.

Then 9/11 happened. Literally overnight, airport rules and regulations changed and they have been changing ever since. Each time the system changes, I have had to adjust my strategy. Now, I am required to arrive at the airport at least one hour before my flight. Immediately upon arrival, the airport notifies you of the threat level for a terrorist attack using a special color code, so you have one hour to think about it. I have noticed that the color usually stays at yellow, which means a "significant" risk of a terrorist attack. After Britain's recent problem, however, the threat level moved to orange, which means "high." I assume that means that I am to go from being significantly scared to fly to highly scared to fly.

Believe me, I am not complaining. I am grateful for anything and everything that can be done to make sure I arrive at my final destination in one piece and with my luggage. It's just that as the rules keep changing, I have to keep adjusting my strategies.

Now, getting through airport security checkpoints without setting off bells, whistles, and alarms takes some planning. I have mostly learned from my mistakes. For example, I discovered that my very favorite black shoes would set off an alarm every time I walked through the metal detection device. When that would happen, out would rush a swarm of uniformed security agents smiling and waving the infamous handheld wand.

Obediently, I would follow orders and stand behind a large glass screen, knowing everyone and his brother could see me. Then they would very politely ask me to assume the "stance." This is a position I found to be very similar to an exercise during my junior high gym class—arms stretched outward, feet spread apart, facing forward. I would stand as still as possible, hold my breath, and allow them to scan my body with the device.

I would pray it would not beep and that no one I knew or knew me was within viewing distance. The agents would then apologize for any inconvenience they may have caused me and send me on my way. Evidently, my favorite black shoes had metal strips in their soles that would set off the alarm.

So I learned not to wear them when I traveled. If I did, I would be forced to take them off, place them in a container, and put them on the belt to go separately through the security scanner, taking up more valuable time.

I changed my strategy. Watching others, I discovered that rubber-soled tennis shoes wouldn't set off the alarm. I got myself a pair of nice, rubber-soled sneakers that I could leave on and walk confidently through the security checkpoint while smiling at the security agents. I called them my airport shoes. It was working really well until the rules changed again.

Now the rules say that all shoes have to come off, regardless.

So, believe it or not, my airport shoes are now more time-consuming than my old black shoes. Unlike my black shoes, you have to relace my airport shoes when you put them back on. So I am back to wearing my old black shoes again.

Airport rules clearly state that knives, scissors, box cutters, other sharp metal objects, and cigarette lighters are not permitted in your carry-on luggage on the plane. These items never really presented a problem for me because I never took them with me in the first place. This new rule, however, the one banning liquids and gel-like substances, has really set me back. My giant economy-sized can of hairspray, hair mousse, hair gel, liquid make-up, lip gloss, hand lotion, face cream, contact solution, shampoo, conditioner, toothpaste, deodorant, and perfume are nonnegotiable travel items. In fact, when I look in my suitcase, almost everything in it is a liquid or gel-like substance. And the no-liquid rule has already gotten me into trouble.

I got busted on my last trip for carrying a bottle of Dasani water in my carry-on. It was a bottle of water they had given me on the plane during my last flight. I had forgotten about it and left it in my bag. Fortunately, I didn't have to assume "the stance" for this infraction but I did get a time-consuming lecture. Now I am forced to do something I absolutely hated to do—check my luggage. If I am lucky enough to have it arrive where I am going, waiting at baggage claim is usually a time-consuming nightmare. So as the rules continue to change, I guess I will just have to continue to adjust my strategy.

Perhaps I can exchange my old black shoes and my airport shoes for a nice pair of ruby slippers. Then all I will have to do is click my heels three times to get where I am going. Better yet, maybe someone will finally invent the one piece of time-saving equipment that I have waited on for years. Then all I will have to say is, "Beam me up, Scotty!" and I can wear any shoes I want.

Infomercials

Have you ever found yourself unable to sleep late at night and resorting to channel surfing on the television? That happened to me the other night. At 3:00 a.m., I was wide-awake, flipping slowly through the channels on the TV in an attempt to find something interesting to watch. Amazingly, on almost every channel, there was someone trying to sell me something.

The first channel showcased two women selling a special facial cream, claiming to make you look up to ten years younger in just one application. I have to admit, the before and after picture of the person who had used the product looked pretty good, but underneath there was this miniscule print that read "these results not typical." It made me wonder why they didn't choose to show the typical results. Wouldn't that make more sense? Anyway, I switched that channel and landed in the midst of a jewelry extravaganza.

Now this looked interesting. A very excited lady was holding up a piece of jewelry and according to her, this item was absolutely the best deal of the evening. It also, by the way, happened to be her personal favorite of the entire show. I watched a little longer and a different piece of jewelry came out on display. Strangely enough, this item was also billed as the best value of the show. Also, after seeing the new item, the excited lady changed her mind and decided it had now become her new personal favorite of the show.

I surfed on to the next channel. Sitting on a chair somewhere in a tropical setting, this young, well-tanned guy told me that if I ordered all his tapes, I could get rich in real estate practically overnight. Now, if this guy knows how to get so rich in the real estate business, why isn't he out selling real estate?

I flipped ahead.

This next commercial really caught my attention. Some lady was selling automatic lighted tweezers for women, guaranteed to painlessly remove all unwanted facial hair and keep it off for months.

I really wasn't interested in the tweezers, but they sure did have some pretty wild before and after pictures. I changed the channel one last time to discover a commercial ironically advertising sleep medication for those having trouble sleeping.

As the little butterfly floated slowly down to land on the lady, she looked as though she immediately drifted right off into a deep, peaceful sleep. No doubt, those phones are ringing off the hook, I thought to myself!

I guess I really shouldn't have been all that surprised to see the number of infomercials on TV that late at night. Television has always had a way of convincing you to try things, even against your better judgment. In fact, I got to thinking about the day many years ago when mother ordered the Vegematic. She had seen a commercial on television. According to the man on TV, the Vegematic did it all—it sliced, it diced, and it chopped with no mess, no fuss. The guy on television showed how you could effortlessly slice a whole ripe tomato perfectly at once with just one downward motion.

That was it—Mama had to have one. My dad called it a "gadget" and said that it was a complete waste of money. After all, that was what they made knives for, wasn't it? Of course, Mama eventually won out and the Vegematic was ordered.

It took several weeks, but the Vegematic finally arrived in the mail. That day, we were all invited into the kitchen for the demonstration. Mama had the new dream machine out on the counter, along with her ripe tomato, positioned and ready to go. Needless to say, the demonstration did not go quite as well as the one done by the TV man. In fact, as I recall, several tomatoes were sacrificed that day in the name of the Vegematic. Later, there were a few more failed attempts on a couple of onions and eventually, the Vegematic was retired to somewhere in the back of a kitchen cabinet, never to be seen again.

I have to admit that ever since the Vegematic experience, I have learned to watch television commercials with some degree of skepticism. By the way, during my late night channel surfing episode, I did restrain from ordering anything.

I do understand, however, that television does have a way of getting to even the toughest of customers. I realized that when our three bottles of HoodiThin Herbal Supplement arrived in the mail the other day. All I will say is that I was not the one who ordered it!

Driving a Hybrid

Learning how to drive a hi-tech vehicle while doing 70 mph on an unfamiliar Texas highway can be more than a little stressful. I know from experience. That is what happened to me last week when I unknowingly rented my first hybrid electric car.

I arrived at the Dallas/Fort Worth Airport early in the afternoon and took the passenger shuttle bus over to the rental car facility. I had a vehicle reserved for the twenty-six mile road trip from the DFW airport to my hotel in Fort Worth.

Exiting the shuttle bus, I followed the signs in the garage to stall 63 where I was told my car would be waiting. I threw my bags in the trunk, opened the door, and climbed into the driver's seat. I noticed that the car was extremely small. Since I usually rent midsized vehicles, I figured they must have been out of them and that this was all they had left.

The usual envelope with the key and contract was hanging on the rearview mirror. I pulled it down and opened it to retrieve the key. Inside the envelope, there was a flat, black object, about the size of a credit card. The object was attached to a tiny chain and it resembled a thin version of a keyless remote for one's car. I figured it must be some type of keychain.

I searched the envelope again for the key, but there wasn't one to be found. I checked the ignition to see if the key happened to have been left there. Where you would normally see the ignition switch, there was only a narrow slot. The slot appeared to be of the size that would match the flat object in the envelope. I looked around at all the other strange, unfamiliar buttons on the dash of this rental car and suddenly realized that I was sitting in one of those fancy new hybrids—an electric car!

My first thought was to return to the counter and tell them that I didn't know how to drive an electric car. Driving between Dallas and Fort Worth, Texas was stressful enough. Doing it in a tiny vehicle with all these foreign buttons and slots would make it even more stressful. I quickly glanced around the car to see if it came with any instructions. There were none.

Surely, I thought, they don't just put people in these cars, say "You'll be fine" and let them drive away without any instructions. But I was already in the car, my bags were in the trunk and I needed to get to Fort Worth.

I decided to go ahead and try to figure it all out.

The first thing I had to learn was how to start the car. After some experimentation, I discovered I had to place the flat, black object from the envelope in the slot and then press a silver button. When I pushed the button the first time, everything on the dashboard lit up like a Christmas tree, including a diagram of a flow chart depicting the inner workings of the engine.

I couldn't hear the engine running so I pushed the silver button once again.

This time the lights on the dash turned off.

I pushed the button a third time and the lights came back on again.

It still didn't sound like the engine was running. So I gently pressed down on the gas pedal with my right foot to see what would happen. The car suddenly moved forward. Fortunately, there was nothing or no one in front of me. That is when I figured out that electric cars don't make much noise when they are started, but they are indeed running.

It took me about ten more minutes, but I also figured out the little knob on the dash that put the car in forward and reverse.

And the other button to put the car in and out of park.

With all this figuring out, you can only imagine how pleased I was when I finally drove the car thirty feet through the garage to the checkout gate. I told the fellow at the gate that I had never driven an electric car, thinking he might become concerned and suggest I exchange cars.

He only smiled and said, "You'll be fine!" So with map in hand, I somehow managed to successfully drive this tiny electric car all the way from the DFW Airport to my hotel in downtown Fort Worth.

Although it was really cold that day, I didn't figure out how to turn on the heat until I had already reached my destination. I never did figure out how to turn on the radio and I was so busy trying to figure out how all the gadgets worked, I drove the entire trip leaning forward. Every muscle in my body ached for two days. However, by the time I returned the little electric car back to the rental garage, I had most of it figured out. In fact, I had grown rather fond of driving it. Best of all, when I checked the gas gauge, it was still showing completely full.

With the price of gas these days, maybe we all should be trying to figure out how to drive these electric cars. You just might not want to take your first test drive on TX-183-W.

Fans Are Cool

Last week, we experienced summer in full force here in southeastern North Carolina. There were a few blistering days, with high temperatures climbing to almost one hundred degrees. People with jobs that require them to work outdoors or those who are not fortunate enough to have air-conditioning in their homes surely must have felt the effects of the sweltering heat.

I was able to stay cool by spending time indoors in the comfort of air-conditioning, something most of us have come to take for granted. Although it would be hard for many of us now to imagine life without it, it really wasn't all that long ago when there was no air-conditioning.

Growing up, I remember many hot summers spent with our windows open trying to stay cool. Instead of air-conditioning, we relied primarily on fans to make life a little more comfortable.

From the beginning of June until early September, a box fan was placed in an open window in our house. It was turned to allow the air to blow air out of the window. I always thought it should be blowing the other direction but was told that doing it this way helped to draw the hot air out of the house, working like an exhaust system.

We also had one large floor fan that blew air inside the house. It was blue in color, made out of metal, and had wheels so you could roll it around. This fan could really put out some wind.

Most summer nights, we slept with our bedroom windows open in order to let the cooler evening air into the house. I would fall asleep listening to the sounds of crickets chirping, tree frogs singing, and the croaking of bullfrogs each night.

On extremely hot nights, the big blue fan was rolled into the bedroom hallway. It would be set on the highest speed and would blow air down the hall. Combined with the open bedroom windows, it helped to create a pleasant draft to make sleeping a bit more comfortable. Sometimes I would take a pillow and blanket to the hallway and sleep on the floor directly in front of the big fan. The humming of that old blue fan would lull me right off to sleep.

Of course back in those days, schools had no air-conditioning. Most schools were not in session during the hot summer months but it still could get extremely warm the last few weeks of May and early June before the school year ended. So most schools were equipped with fans to help the kids and teachers get through those last few weeks of warm weather.

Donnie Garner was one of my husband's classmates at Hope Mills School. Donnie's father, Curtis Garner, donated two large fans to Hope Mills School when Donnie and his brother Eddie were students there in elementary school. Eddie Garner told me that his father built special encasements around the large fans with protective wire to ensure that children could not get their fingers through to the spinning blades and be injured. The fans created a gust of wind that helped keep the classrooms more comfortable on those extremely warm days when school was still in session.

It seems there was an agreement that the fans were to remain in Eddie and Donnie's classrooms each year. Mike said he always felt lucky because he was in Donnie's classes every year and was able to reap the benefits of one of the big fans as it moved through the grades with Donnie.

The first time I remember getting in an air-conditioned car was a 1968 Buick belonging to J. Hollis Fields, a good friend of our family. Mr. Fields was waiting in that car one summer day for his wife, Janet. She was shopping for groceries at the old A&P Store on Raeford Road.

We were sitting in our car waiting for my mother who also happened to be shopping at the A&P. We were in an Impala that was not air-conditioned. It was a really hot day and we had the windows rolled down.

Mr. Fields drove up beside us in his Buick and motioned for me to come and sit in his car. I got out of our car and climbed into the air-conditioned Buick. I couldn't believe how cool it was and how good that air-conditioning felt inside his car on that hot summer day. From that moment on, we began asking the question—when will we get a car just like Mr. Fields?

We finally did. My dad bought that old '68 Buick from Mr. Fields a few years later. It wasn't too long after that our old box fan and big blue metal floor fan were replaced with a central air-conditioning system in our house and the windows were closed year round.

Today, I seldom open the windows in our home. I still have fans but they are the kind you attach to the ceiling. But it seems that even with the comfort of my air conditioner on really hot summer nights, I can't resist the temptation of falling asleep to the humming sound of the fan in my room set on the highest speed.

I guess you could say that I will always be a fan of a fan. You see, I still think fans are rather cool.

Part VI

But Mostly the Other

AND NOW THE REST OF THE STORIES

Kidney Stones

I never personally experienced a kidney stone and from what I hear, I sincerely hope I never do. I have been very fortunate in that respect. I understand that they can be very serious and are often quite painful. But last week, I felt like I did get to experience a kidney stone sort of vicariously as my sister-in-law was diagnosed with one and I speak with her on a daily basis.

Rebecca called and told me that she had not been feeling well. She had complained about a growing pain in her back. The clincher came the evening she and my brother went with a group of friends to the Rock-Ola Cafe.

She said that she was in so much pain she couldn't even make it through dinner. She finally ended up in the emergency room at Pinehurst Medical Center that evening. After a couple of tests and a CAT scan, she was diagnosed with a kidney stone that was approximately five millimeters in size.

After her examination, she was given a strainer, some instructions, and told to go home and drink lots of water and cranberry juice. According to the doctor, it was just a matter of time for the stone to eventually pass and she would need to wait it out. So that is exactly what she did. She went home and waited patiently for several days. She drank lots of water and juice. But nothing happened. I know because every day we would talk on the phone and I would get an update.

After a week, I could tell she was beginning to grow impatient. Finally, she called and told me she was tired of waiting around. She decided she was going to try a couple of ideas she had come up with in order to see if she could expedite the passing of the stone.

Her first idea was to simply try to exercise it out. Since sitting around waiting didn't seem to be working, she figured if she moved around and shook her body hard enough it might cause the stone to move on through her system. Rebecca pulled out an old exercise video and worked out to Turbo Jam—a high powered kickboxing kind of exercise routine that requires some major body movement. She tried hard but the report I received back the next day was that the Turbo Jam session didn't work. The stone still had not passed and that as a result, she was planning to try her other idea.

This idea was to cut the grass on the riding lawn mower. She thought it might vibrate and shake the stubborn stone loose, causing it to move on through and exit out of her system. So she cranked up the lawn mower and mowed her front lawn. I didn't want to say anything but this was very similar to the procedure my brother used on her nineteen years ago when she was a week overdue with my niece. In order to get her to begin labor, he put her in his pickup truck and drove her up and down a bumpy road over some railroad tracks. It didn't work then with my niece and the lawn mower ride didn't work this time with the kidney stone, either.

Now the little bit of experience I happen to have had with kidney stones comes from my husband having experienced one a year or so ago. It was excruciatingly painful for him, but the stone just seemed to pass on its own due time. When it finally did, we examined it closely and decided that it resembled a small dark sandspur. Therefore, I had already warned my sister-in-law to look out for something that may look like a tiny dark jagged rock or burr.

Finally, a couple of days ago, my sister-in-law called me extremely excited. She had discovered something unusual that she thought might be the kidney stone that had been causing her so much trouble. She was concerned, however, because she thought the object resembled a teeny little arrow head instead of a sandspur. She said my brother had checked it out and he thought it looked more like a cornflake than a kidney stone.

I reminded her that I had only seen one in my life and they had seen none. So maybe kidney stones come in different shapes. Maybe they can be shaped like sandspurs, arrowheads, and cornflakes, and anything else for that matter.

Anyway, the object in question was dropped into a clear plastic baggy and taken to the urologist for further inspection. Sure enough, it was the infamous kidney stone we had all been waiting to pass for the last two weeks.

I am not sure if it was the Turbo Jam super exercise routine, the twelve glasses of water a day, the cranberry juice, the lawn mower ride, or just the course of nature itself that finally did the trick. But the stone did pass and I can tell you that we are all feeling much better as a result.

Horses on Main Street

Another Friday afternoon and traffic, as usual, is bumper to bumper on Main Street in Hope Mills. On the side of the road, I notice a bright yellow diamond-shaped sign depicting a picture of a horse with a red diagonal line drawn through it—the symbolic representation for "No horses allowed."

Stuck in traffic, I can only smile trying to visualize the same number of horses as there are vehicles, nose to rear, waiting for the light to turn green at Trade and Main.

With all the traffic in town, there really is no need to question why they do not allow horses on Main Street. So why the "No horses allowed" sign?

As a horse lover myself, my curiosity was sparked and I decided to do a little investigation. I was amazed at what I learned.

Evidently, there was a time not too long ago when horses frequented Main Street and a lot of other streets in the town of Hope Mills. Every Sunday for about twenty years, 1965 until 1985, local area horse lovers would gather for a day of horseback riding fun. Others would join the local area riders on these Sunday excursions, coming from as far away as Clinton, Dunn, and Autryville. At times, the group totaled as many as twenty horses and riders.

The banks of the beautiful Rockfish Creek and scenic wooded areas within and surrounding our community provided perfect riding trails and several local horse stables provided easy access to horses. There were stables located at Permastone Lake, Lakewood, and on Church Street where Creek Bend subdivision now exists. Horses could be rented for as little as two dollars an hour and sixteen dollars for an entire day.

Recently, I met up with some of the former Hope Mills area horse riders. Johnny Tarpley, John Brown, Ping Cole, and Randy Fowler were all members of the "Hole-in-the-Wall" gang, so nicknamed because they would often meet at Randy Fowler's place located down a hill off Camden Road referred to as "the hole."

The area is now Gray Fox Stables and home to many truly magnificent horses. According to Tarpley, for two decades, horseback riding in Hope Mills was a major social event. Tarpley's horse was named Sundance, a beautiful Appaloosa well known throughout the community. John Brown described Sundance as closely resembling the horse once ridden by the notorious Wild Bill Hickok.

According to Ping Cole, the horseback riders had established riding places, trails, and crossings that were given their own special names. For example, where the South Main subdivision now exists, there was a large open area known as "The Hayfield." This was a gathering place for the horseback riders to begin their rides. They would leave the "The Hayfield" and ride their horses down Main Street—yes, down Main Street—to meet in the open lot across from Hope Mills Lake where the BB&T now exists. With their horses tethered to trees, they would spend time socializing with friends and other visitors to Hope Mills Lake.

Crossing places on Rockfish Creek had their own special names as well. For the more daring riders, there was "Benny's Slide" located off Cameron Road. According to John Brown, there you could test your bravery and riding skills by sliding down a steep, slippery clay slope dropping off into Rockfish Creek. It was definitely not for the faint of heart! "Johnson's Crossing" which was also located off Cameron Road, provided another creek crossing that was challenging but not quite as difficult.

I listened as the gang reminisced about the horses, twenty years later, still remembering each one by name and reputation. Lady, Bitsy, Tony, Diver, Sundance, and Thunderbolt were among the horses that provided hours of fun and a collection of priceless memories for the Hole-in-the-Wall gang. Thunderbolt was the horse everyone agreed presented the greatest challenge to the riders. According to the gang, Ping Cole was the only one that could successfully ride him. Ping would occasionally trick his buddies into trying to ride, but all the others would quickly end up on the ground when Thunderbolt, true to his name, decided to bolt.

The Hole-in-the-Wall gang no longer exists but the established friendships and memories from days gone by do. Many of the open fields, pastures, and trails frequented by the horseback riders have been replaced by housing developments, apartment complexes, stores, and parking lots. I guess this is all in the name of progress and, of course, horseback riding is no longer allowed on Main Street.

I believe, however, that with a little foresight and planning, there are still areas remaining throughout our community that have the potential to be developed into beautiful horseback riding trails. And with gasoline prices hovering around $2.75 a gallon, riding a hayburner may not be such a bad transportation alternative. Hay averages around $4.75 a bale. Grass is free. Throw in a scoop full of oats each day and your horse is fueled up for a week. Wouldn't it be great if one day in the future, we could have some safe, well-planned places within our community for horse lovers to take their Sunday afternoon rides?

Perhaps this would inspire the "Hole-in-the-Wall" gang to saddle up and ride again.

Just not down Main Street!

The Sandy Hook Tragedy

The horrific act that occurred last Friday at a Connecticut elementary school has once again left behind grief-stricken families and a devastated nation shaken beyond belief. The senseless loss of twenty young lives, and six adults responsible for their care and education, hits home to all of us.

With very few exceptions, we have all been students in school. More importantly, we can all relate at some level as a parent, grandparent, aunt, uncle, brother, or sister. We continue to ask ourselves why this happened. As a nation, we struggle for answers to what appears to be an escalation in the number of such tragic incidents of mass murder.

The Sandy Hook tragedy hit home on a personal note for me. As a former elementary school principal, I found myself trying to imagine the events that morning at Sandy Hook Elementary School. My mind's eye envisioned a building and classrooms decorated with children's artwork for the holidays. I could see the principal moving through the bustle of the front office as she prepared for routine morning announcements, in her hand a list of reminders about important activities and events for the day.

I envisioned teachers in their classroom counting heads, taking attendance and lunch count, listening to important stories their students were eager to share and double checking materials for the day's lessons. I envisioned the children, a little more excited than usual because of the upcoming holidays. Everyone was at school, without much greater worry than making sure they were all settling in for another day of learning. The rest of the events are the unimaginable for me.

From the news accounts, we hear the principal gave her life attempting to stop the crazed gunman. Teachers sacrificed their lives attempting to protect their children. I understand all that because that was their most important job—to keep the children safe.

At this most sad time, our thoughts and prayers turn to the victims of this senseless tragedy, their families, and the community of Newtown. Let us also remember all our nation's educators that returned to school last Monday as they support, guide, and reassure their students and work to keep them safe.

No student, ever, should have to worry about being safe at school.

No teacher, principal, or school employee should have to worry about being safe at work.

No parent should have to worry about their child's safety while at school.

No community should ever have to grieve, as they are grieving over the tragic events in Newtown.

School Soup

With the onset of cold weather, I've pulled out my old soup pot and started putting it to use. This is the time of year that I really enjoy making homemade soup. As far as I am concerned, there is nothing better than a hot bowl of soup to warm you up on a chilly day.

I know how to make many different kinds of soups. In fact, I have a few recipe books that are devoted entirely to soup. Nonetheless, in the old metal pot on my stove, you will usually only find one kind simmering under its lid, "School Soup." At least that is what it is affectionately referred to in our family. And of course there is a story behind how it got its name.

When I was a kid, I always looked forward to Fridays at school. Not only was it the day before the weekend, it was also the day when the ladies in the cafeteria served vegetable soup. We would always joke that the reason they served soup on Fridays was because they made it with the leftover vegetables scraped from our plates on Monday through Thursday.

I remember one kid in my class who claimed that they threw the leftover vegetables in a big pot of dishwater and that's how they made the soup.

Still, it was the best soup in the world to me.

What was really great was that you could smell the soup all over the school when it was cooking. On really cold Friday mornings, it was even hard to concentrate in class. At lunchtime, we would go through the line with our trays and balance our little plastic bowl of soup to the lunch table. Usually, the soup was served with a cheese sandwich or sometimes a peanut butter and honey sandwich.

I guess my mother heard so much talk at home about the soup they served at school that she decided one day to make a trip to visit the cafeteria workers. She asked them if they would be willing to share the recipe for the soup. They did and she wrote it down on a small index card. Later, she began making the soup for our family. For lack of a better name, we referred to it as "School Soup."

When I left for college, I would return home for visits on the weekends. Mama would always call ahead and ask what I wanted for supper when I arrived on Friday night. The answer was always the same, "School Soup." I knew I would smell it simmering on the stove the minute I walked in the door.

There is something comforting about the smell of homemade soup. It was no accident that the authors titled their best-selling book of comfort stories, Chicken Soup for the Soul. f I were ever to write a book of comforting stories, I think I might title mine, School Soup for the Soul.

You won't find the recipe for School Soup in a store-bought book. You won't see it featured on any restaurant menu. The recipe is scribbled on an old index card tucked safely away in my wooden recipe box. I don't have to look at the recipe card anymore though. I have made School Soup so often that I have it memorized. As soup weather has arrived and at this time of Thanksgiving, I would like to share this special recipe with you. Here's wishing you and your family a wonderful Thanksgiving.

School Soup

1 48 oz. can tomato juice

1 lb. freshly ground beef

1 bag frozen mixed vegetables

2 potatoes, diced

2 med. onions, diced

2 teaspoons salt

1 teaspoon Worcestershire sauce

Bring tomato juice to a boil. Slowly add crumbled ground beef. Cook until beef is separated. Add onions, mixed vegetables, potatoes, salt and Worcestershire sauce.

Cook over medium heat until vegetables are tender, stirring occasionally.

Add more salt if desired.

Putt-Putt Birthday Girl

According to a recent news account, Putt-Putt is returning to its Cumberland County roots. Even better, Millstone Village in Hope Mills has been chosen as the location for the brand new Putt-Putt Fun Center. That is really good news for Hope Mills.

I think Millstone Village will be the perfect site for the new Putt-Putt facility. After all, Putt-Putt has always been about bringing together families and friends for wholesome fun and entertainment. I did have to smile when I read where insurance executive Jimmy Smith, one of the investors in the venture, said that he and all the other partners still have pictures of kids' birthday parties at Putt-Putt. That is because I doubt there are many people that have more special memories about those Putt-Putt birthday parties than me.

You see, one summer, I was the "Putt-Putt Birthday Girl." It was my job to coordinate all the birthday parties at Putt-Putt for the kids and their families.

Like many people my age, I grew up playing Putt-Putt with friends and family. But a much deeper affiliation with Putt-Putt developed during my early high school days. Throughout my sophomore, junior, and senior years of high school, I was the regular babysitter for Don Clayton's two grandchildren, Dave and Scott Lloyd.

Don Clayton was a Fayetteville businessman and the founder of Putt-Putt.

When three other Clayton grandchildren came along—Amy, Hannah, and Lisa Clayton—I became their babysitter too. In fact, I spent so much time with all the Clayton grandchildren they often joked affectionately that Lisa, the last of the five grandchildren, was named after me.

Needless to say, I spent a lot of time around Putt-Putt and related activities. I even traveled with the family to one of the National Putt-Putt Championship tournaments. My job was to watch the kids while their parents spent the day working on the televised event. After my senior year of high school, I was offered the job of "Putt-Putt Birthday Girl" during the summer prior to my leaving to attend East Carolina University.

My job was to coordinate the birthday parties—from the balloons to the birthday hats—and to ensure that all the kids had a safe and fun experience. I tried to make sure each birthday party was special for the kids.

I remember part of my job as "Birthday Girl" was to drive from the Putt-Putt golf course on Bragg Boulevard to Superior Bakery on Hope Mills Road to pick up the cake before each party.

It was a long drive and I wondered why they didn't choose a bakery that was closer. I figured it out when I tasted the first birthday cake. As it happens, Don Clayton's grandkids grew up. I went on to college to study and eventually become a teacher. I guess I figured that if I could organize fifteen four-year-olds armed with golf clubs, golf balls, and water balloons, teaching school would be like a piece of Putt-Putt birthday cake.

Margaret

Early Saturday morning, my neighbor called to let me know that Margaret, his beloved wife and my friend and neighbor, had passed away. Margaret had been in failing health for the past few weeks and we all knew the prognosis wasn't good. Regardless, the news of her passing came hard. Good friends are irreplaceable and I considered Margaret Thompson to be a very good friend.

I first met Margaret when I moved to Hope Mills ten years ago. She lived next door and came over to introduce herself to me one day while I was walking around in my yard. We chatted across the fence for a while and I remember that she commented to me that she thought my house would look better if it were painted gray. I wasn't sure what to think of that comment at the time. Later, when I got to know Margaret, I learned that was just Margaret—a person who knew what she liked and would tell you what she thought. If you agreed with Margaret, that was fine.

If you disagreed with her, well that was perfectly fine too.

Margaret soon became a friend I could call to talk to at any time and about anything. In fact, we talked either in person or on the phone almost on a daily basis. During our conversations, it was clear that she was able to see the humor in just about everything.

Margaret was a natural and gifted musician. She loved playing the organ and played it beautifully. She had a flare for fashion, an eye for decorating, a love of gardening, and a special personal style all of her own. In fact, whenever you saw Margaret, she was always dressed up to the nines. Whether eating breakfast at Becky's Café, attending a town board meeting, or out in the yard pulling weeds, Margaret would always be dressed in her Sunday best.

One day, I actually questioned her as to why she stayed so dressed up all the time. Her explanation was clear and made me stop and think. Margaret told me she grew up poor. She and her family lived on a farm located far out in the country. Growing up, she said, people always tried to stay dressed up just in case one of their neighbors might happen by, making the long trip into town that day.

"If they saw you and had room in the car, they would stop and ask if you wanted to ride up to town," she told me.

"You always had to be ready to go to town." That was my good friend Margaret, always dressed and ready to go to town.

And by the way, I did paint my house gray and it did look better, just like my friend Margaret said.

Neighbors

You never really know when you may need a little neighborly help. I was working in my kitchen the other morning when I heard the loudest noise one could ever imagine and it seemed to be coming from my neighbor's house. The noise was shrill, like the squeal of some poor wounded animal in distress and was accompanied by the occasional rat-tat-tat of what sounded like a loud, overbearing snare drum.

I raced out the front door to investigate and found my bewildered neighbor standing in her front yard staring up at the roof of her house. As the noise continued to grow louder and shriller, my neighbor explained to me that her husband was out of town for the day; she was home alone and wasn't sure what was causing the noise or what she should do. To tell you the truth, neither was I. Now, we were both standing in the yard, looking somewhat bewildered and listening to the strange noise coming from the roof of her house.

Soon another neighbor appeared in the yard. He must have heard all the commotion from across the street and come to help. After a brief discussion about the strange sound, he went into the house and climbed up into the attic where the horrible sound seemed to be originating. After a few minutes, the noise abruptly came to a stop.

Neighbor number two emerged from the small hole leading to the attic, perspiring from the heat but with a smile on his face. He informed us that a worn-out attic fan was to blame for creating the terrible noise and that he was sure he had fixed the problem, at least temporarily. Relieved, we had a good laugh, said our good-byes, and went about our business of the day.

Reflecting back, I think about how great it is to live in a small community where neighbors are often your first responders in times of need. As a child, I learned the importance of having good neighbors. My family knew all our neighbors and we watched out for each other. All the adults in the neighborhood kept a watchful eye on all the neighborhood children. If something seemed wrong, your neighbors noticed and let you know.

If someone in your family was sick, your neighbors brought food. If the newspaper stayed in the driveway a little too long, your neighbors called to check on you or brought it to your door just to make certain everything was okay. Not only did your neighbors wave as you passed by, they smiled and called you by your name.

Probably the most important lesson I learned from those neighborly experiences was that in order to have a good neighbor, one must first be a good neighbor. All those years ago, we didn't have a fancy green sign on our street to proclaim "Neighborhood Watch," but we had a "Neighborhood Watch" in the truest sense of the word.

All too often in this busy world, neighbors do not even know each other by name, much less see themselves as responsible for looking out for one another. Living in a small town like Hope Mills affords us the opportunity to get to know one another and to become good neighbors. I believe we should grasp that opportunity and try to make the very most of it.

Funny as it may seem, I somehow feel a little safer, settled, and more secure after my neighborhood "strange noise" incident. It's comforting to know that you live in a community where neighbors look out for neighbors, and if you are ever in need of a little neighborly help, it is just around the corner!

Priorities

What would you do if you thought you were suddenly going to lose your home and everything you had worked for all your life? It's amazing how fast your priorities surface when you are forced to make quick decisions about what is important to you and what you value most in life. It actually happened a few weeks ago in our family.

My sister-in-law, Rebecca, had called earlier in the day to tell me she was coming over to visit. While I was waiting for her to arrive, the phone rang.

To my surprise, it was an out-of-breath Rebecca. She told me that there was a fire raging in the woods near their subdivision in Hoke County where she and my brother, Drew, live.

She said she could see the thick, black smoke billowing in the sky, moving steadily in the direction of their home. The firefighters were having difficulty controlling the blaze because of the twenty-mile-per-hour winds. Their neighborhood had received word that if the fire jumped one more street, the entire subdivision would have to be immediately evacuated.

I knew there had been warnings issued earlier in the day that drought conditions, combined with high wind and low humidity, made for an extremely high fire hazard. Never in my wildest dreams, however, would I have imagined a wildfire threatening a subdivision in a neighboring county. However, I could hear the panic in Rebecca's voice.

I asked her what she planned to do. She told me that my brother had already prepared the truck in case they had to leave. Then, he went across the street to help a neighbor who has a young child and a husband deployed to Iraq.

That was enough information for me. Mike and I jumped into the car and drove to Hoke County. When we neared the subdivision, I could smell the fire. Ashes were falling on the car and it looked as if it were snowing. You could actually see the red glow of the blaze in the distance.

Rebecca was standing at the door when we pulled in the drive. As we entered the house, I saw dozens of family photographs, normally hanging on the walls throughout the house, stacked on a counter by the door.

I glanced around at all the furniture still in place. Then I looked at Rebecca and asked, "What else are you going to take if you have to evacuate? What about money, jewelry, or insurance papers?"

"I don't know," she said. "When I heard we might have to leave, I just began grabbing all the family pictures off of the wall."

As it turns out, the firefighters were finally able to contain the fire in Hoke County. And fortunately, the subdivision did not have to be evacuated. But that whole experience caused me to pause and think about priorities in life.

If you were given notice that you might lose your home and everything you had worked for in a matter of hours, what would you do first? My brother Drew got the truck ready to take his family to safety and then ran to help his neighbor.

That doesn't surprise me.

Of all your worldly possessions, what would be the first thing you would think to take with you? For Rebecca, it wasn't money, jewelry, or insurance papers. Rebecca's first thought was to grab her priceless family photographs.

And that doesn't surprise me either.

Superstitions

On New Year's Eve, I was in the kitchen putting away some groceries. Mike was on his way out the door. He suddenly turned to remind me that I might want to go ahead and take care of any laundry that needed tending.

"Remember, you can't do laundry tomorrow because it is New Year's Day," he said. "It's bad luck."

"Where did you hear that?" I asked with some amusement.

"I have heard it all my life."Now surely he doesn't actually believe that washing clothes on the first day of the New Year will bring bad luck, I thought to myself. It's just a silly superstition.

Then I turned back to the task at hand.

Who had time to think about doing laundry anyway?

I was too busy preparing for the New Year's Day meal.

One by one, I removed the black-eyed peas, side meat, and collard greens from a plastic grocery bag. I placed them in a row on the counter.

Next I opened the cabinet and pulled out a large pot and a frying pan. I placed the side meat in the pan and filled the pot with cold water for the peas. At that point, I wasn't sure what else was on the menu for New Year's Day. But without a doubt, black-eyed peas and collard greens were going to be the featured dishes.

Everyone knows that eating collards and black-eyed peas on the first day of the New Year brings good luck.

The peas represent change and the collards represent dollars. Eating both will help you to accumulate more wealth during the coming year. This year, I decided to double up on the collards. Superstition or not, I have eaten collards and black-eyed peas on New Year's Day all of my life.

I decided to look up the definition of superstition in the Merriam-Webster Dictionary. According to the dictionary, a superstition is a belief or practice resulting from ignorance, fear of the unknown, or trust in magic or chance.

Some superstitions are cultural, passed on from generation to generation such as the tradition of eating collards and black-eyed peas on New Year's. Others may be more personal in nature, such as having a lucky number or carrying a lucky object around in your pocket.

I guess I grew up hearing lots of superstitions.

However, not doing any laundry on New Year's Day wasn't one of them.

I did hear that if your nose itches, someone is coming to visit you.

If your ears are burning, someone is talking about you.

If your right palm itches, you are going to receive some money.

If your left palm itches, you are going to have to pay someone some money. It is bad luck to open an umbrella inside the house.

It is also bad luck to exit out of a different door from the one you entered.

Now, it's not that I actually believe any of these old superstitions.

It is just that I prefer not taking any unnecessary chances, that's all. So any time a black cat crosses my path, I use my finger to draw an X three times in the air. That will reverse the bad luck. In fact, I will even make an X in the air three times for a black and white cat, as long as it is mostly black. I also knock on wood, whenever I mention good fortune to keep from losing it.

If I spill salt, I throw a pinch of it back over my left shoulder.

And I refuse to walk under a ladder, period. In fact, at Home Depot the other day, I wouldn't even stick my head up under one that was blocking a shelf in order to check the price of an item. I asked the salesman to please move it out of the way. He smiled and then gladly obliged.

But who knows? After reading the definition of superstition in the dictionary, I may decide to rethink some of these practices. Until then, I have a wishbone drying on my kitchen counter waiting to be pulled. And you can be sure I will pick up a penny on the sidewalk if I see one.

Of course, that is as long as it is facing heads up!

The Old Barn

No doubt about it, life can get a little hectic at times. I know mine certainly does. For example, in the past two weeks I have been to California and back, twice. To me, it isn't all that much fun maneuvering through busy airports, sitting for hours in cramped airplane seats, and gobbling down hotdogs in between flights at the airport. Hotels aren't all that much fun either, especially the last two where I stayed. I can assure you that neither were the Ritz Carlton. Also, driving rental cars in unfamiliar cities can be nerve-racking.

So, as you can imagine, when I finally do get home, just the opportunity to sleep in my own bed is a real treat. I think everyone's life can get to be a little hectic and stressful at times. That is why it is so important to have a stress reliever in your life—something that simply helps you to calm down and relax.

It is important to have something that helps get your mind off work and day-to-day problems. For some people, I think golf must provide that avenue to relaxation. For other people, gardening or cooking may be their stress buster. Some people like to read for relaxation. And other people may find fishing to have that calming effect. Not me. I like spending a little time at the old barn.

The barn is a one-hundred-year-old smokehouse that has been somewhat renovated in the past few years in order to accommodate the fifty bales of hay that must be stored each winter for the horse. It also has to provide storage space for a lot of other food as well—cat food, dog food, horse food, and chicken food to be specific.

Attached to the barn on one side is a stall with a window. That is where ole Butter Bean, the horse, can stick in her big head from time to time to check out what is going on. When they first see it, most people tell me that they think the barn resembles the little wooden shack that Jed Clampett built behind his mansion in Beverly Hills—the shack that Granny preferred living in.

There is a sign hanging at the barn that reads "Critter Crossing" because the barn, the surrounding pasture, and adjacent woods serve as home to many of God's creatures. There are squirrels, raccoons, opossums, and a variety of colorful birds that make their home in the trees and wooded area that border the pasture. The barn also serves as home to Weasel, the wise old barn cat, her kittens, and a proud little bantam rooster named Junior Jr.

Junior Jr. weighs a little over a pound and is only about eight inches tall, but what he lacks in size, he makes up in attitude. His feathers reflect a multitude of colors, and he has an impressive strut anyone has to admire as he makes his way each day around the barnyard, through the pasture, and into the woods to scratch for bugs and worms. Junior Jr. was raised with the barn cats, so of course he thinks he is a cat!

When you call "kitty, kitty," the cats come running through the pasture, followed closely on their heels by Junior Jr., the rooster. When they all reach the barn, Junior Jr. quickly flies up on the railing of the porch, wanting to be the first one picked up and petted. While the cats gobble down their Meow Mix, I pick up Junior Jr., and feed him cracked corn from my hand.

On the porch of the barn, there are two old wooden rocking chairs, angled on either side of a makeshift coffee table that was created by placing a round stepping stone atop an old plastic milk crate. The rocking chairs have a distinctive squeak to them when you rock. Late afternoon, after all the animals are checked, fed, and watered, it is time to sit down for a few minutes and rock, watch the sun go down behind the treetops, and reflect on what is really important in my life. Of course, I always end up with a few cats crossing over my lap, each wanting a turn at being scratched and petted. Early evening as the sun begins to settle down over the horizon, like clockwork, Rocky the squirrel scurries home to a little hole in the old oak tree next to the barn and Junior Jr. makes his way up high in the rafters and crows everyone good night.

It is at that very moment, it seems like all the stress and the worries of life temporarily melt away. I dearly love spending time down at that old barn. So maybe it is only fitting that my dad nicknamed me Ellie Mae when I was growing up.

Drive-In Days

The year was 1969 but somehow it seems like only yesterday. I remember it was very early on a Saturday evening just before dark. I was over at my friend's house next door. There was no school the next day and she had invited me to a sleepover. After we finished dinner, her parents announced that we were all going to a drive-in movie. It was almost dark, so we began to hustle to get ready.

My friend and I grabbed pillows and blankets. Her mom popped a bunch of corn and placed it in a brown paper A&P grocery bag. We loaded up in the family station wagon and headed to the Midway Drive-In on Bragg Boulevard.

When we arrived at the drive-in, we pulled up to the booth to pay our admission fee. The man at the ticket window counted heads and asked ages. As we pulled in, I remember the excitement of seeing the cars already parked facing the huge blank screen, waiting for the movie to begin.

Finally, after circling around the lot a few times looking for a good spot, the wagon was parked. Following a little discussion about which ones belonged to us, the speakers were pulled down from the posts and hung on the windows.

As it turns out, the movie playing that night was True Grit. It was a cowboy-western featuring John Wayne and Glenn Campbell. John Wayne played "Rooster Cogburn," a one-eyed marshal, and Glenn Campbell played a Texas Ranger. Together they assist a young girl trying to find her father's killer.

John Wayne would later win a Best Actor Oscar for his performance in this movie.

As the movie began, my girlfriend and I somehow managed to climb out of the rear window of the station wagon and on to the top of the vehicle. It was atop this perch that we watched True Grit, eating our way through an entire A&P bag full of popcorn.

Unfortunately, the Midway Drive-In on Bragg Boulevard no longer exists.

The old A&P grocery stores are now closed.

Even so, I can still go back to that special time in my life through my memories.

Who knows? Maybe that drive-in experience in 1969 had something to do with why I remain such a John Wayne fan today.

Paul the Perfectionist

Sometimes it is fun to step out of your daily routine and try something different for a change. This past week, I got to try out a new job. I had the opportunity to work as a carpenter's helper. Frankly, I would have preferred the title Carpentry Associate or maybe even Executive Assistant to the carpenter. But Paul just kept on referring to me as his helper. By the end of the week, I can say that I learned some things I didn't know about carpentry work. I also learned that it isn't always easy to work with a perfectionist.

Paul is the one person we usually call when we have any major project around the house. Paul is a master carpenter and he can build or repair just about anything and everything. Whatever he does, he always does extremely well. When it comes to his work, Paul is what I would call a total perfectionist. I think that must be why he usually prefers to work alone.

I jokingly asked Paul if he had brought anyone to help him this trip. He told me he brought his best two helpers—his right hand and his left hand. Then he showed me a wooden clamp. He said that clamp would hold the other end of a board straighter and steadier than nine out of ten people. What's more, he said, the clamp never complains, always shows up for work on time and doesn't have to be paid.

I couldn't argue with that. This particular trip, however, Paul agreed to allow me to help out a little. I listened to Paul as we worked and he taught me some rather interesting things.

For example, did you know that if you dig a hole on a waning moon and then try to refill the hole with the same dirt, there won't be enough dirt to fill the hole? At least that is what Paul says.

Paul also says if you dig a hole on a growing moon, you can place the same dirt back into the hole and it will completely fill it up. I told him I didn't believe it. He swears it is true.

What I didn't tell him is that I plan to try it myself the next time the moon is right.

There was something else I learned from Paul that surprised me. Did you know that an eight foot two by four isn't really eight feet long, two inches thick or four inches wide? That's what they call it and that's how they sell it, but those aren't the exact measurements. I didn't believe that either until I saw Paul measure the board. It may be really close but you still will usually have to make adjustments. And when you do, you measure twice and cut once.

I also learned this week that you never, ever let someone else select your boards. According to Paul, if you want the very best boards, you must always take the time to go and pick them out yourself. Turn them over one by one and check underneath. Most of the time, you will find the attractive side of the board is turned up. The knots and imperfections are hidden on the side that is turned down that you can't see.

Now I told Paul that I did believe that one because that is how I shop for strawberries. It seems that the pretty side is usually up and you have to turn the carton over to see if the bottoms of the berries are in good shape before you buy them.

Working with Paul, I found out that it is not always easy to assist a perfectionist. They expect you to perfectly assist. Watching their eyes, however, helps because you can anticipate what they are thinking. That, in turn, helps you to plan your next move without getting into any problems.

For example, Paul picked up a really heavy board and carried it to exactly where he wanted it. I could tell it was a heavy board because of the strained look on his face. While he was putting it down, I noticed he was staring over at his nail gun which was at least a good fifteen feet away. I read his mind. He was thinking he should have placed the nail gun within reach before moving the board. Seizing the opportunity, I quickly jumped up and ran to get the nail gun.

Before picking it up, however, I remembered that it is also best to ask just to be on the safe side. "Hey! Paul! You want me to hand you your nail gun?" Turns out I was right!

When you work with a perfectionist like Paul, you should try to listen to their conversations. That will also give you some insight into what they may be thinking. They tend to talk mostly to themselves. But if they are mumbling under their breath, I found the best thing to do is to not interrupt and just remain quiet.

This week has been a really fun, learning experience for me. But I think it's time that I return to my day job. And I think Paul would think that would be a perfectly good idea.

Multitasking

For the past thirty minutes, I have had the phone glued to my ear, listening to some rather nice symphony music. I was placed on hold by a Delta Airlines agent who was working to reissue a ticket for my morning flight to Cincinnati. I had just discovered via the internet that I could leave an hour and a half later in the morning, still make my connection in Atlanta, and arrive in Cincinnati at the same time as the earlier flight.

With the phone strategically balanced on my left shoulder, I held it in place pressing down with my left ear in order to free up my hands. I needed them because I was responding to e-mails that had piled up during the week and required attention. Working on my plane ticket and answering my e-mail, I watched the Dr. Phil show out of one corner of my eye as he tried to straighten out some guy with what was obviously a pretty serious gambling problem.

As the Dr. Phil show concluded, all my e-mails were completed and the agent had my ticket reissued for the later flight. So I moved on to my next set of tasks—folding laundry and talking to my sister-in-law on the phone while keeping my eye on the meatballs baking in the oven for my Christmas party on Saturday. This time, however, I decided to switch the phone over to my right ear in order to give my left ear and shoulder a break.

It is called multitasking; working on multiple things simultaneously in order to try to get more done in less time. Lately, I have found that I have to resort to doing it for at least part of my day, every day. If everything I did was done in isolation, I do not believe that there would be enough hours in a day to get it all completed. Whether it be returning business calls on my cell phone while grocery shopping or sending instant messages to my friends on the computer while paying the bills, I find that in order to get everything done, I sometimes have to double up or even triple up on what I am doing at any one time.

I often practice my multitasking skills by playing games to try to sharpen my ability. My morning test is usually attempting to unload the dishwasher, put away the dishes, and feed the dogs before the coffee finishes brewing. The ability to multitask requires a general awareness of everything in your environment. It is probably best left to tasks that do not require any deep thought or concentration.

Even if it takes longer, some people still prefer to focus all of their attention on one task and do it well before moving on to others. It can drive us that are into multitasking nuts. For example, I was in the drugstore the other day and needed a new battery. After searching unsuccessfully for a while, I decided to ask someone at the checkout counter for help.

There was quite a long line waiting to check out and I didn't want to be rude and break in line. I thought maybe I could catch the cashier's eye and he could answer my question while he finished up with the customer he was waiting on.

But this fellow was obviously a single-tasker. One sure sign always gives them away; he refused to make eye contact with me. People who are only able to single-task often avoid having to multitask by not making eye contact.

So, I stood off to the side a little in line thinking that would get his attention. It didn't even faze this single-tasker. Keeping his eyes glued on the cash register, he continued working away, pretending he didn't see me. I moved up closer.

He never looked up. I watched as slowly one by one, each customer ahead of me completed their transactions at the register. I decided it would be quicker to go back and continue searching for the hidden batteries myself than to try to get this guy to do two things at once.

For whatever reason, I think women are better than men when it comes to multitasking. And I think kids are better at it than adults. Kids can do their homework, talk on the phone, listen to music, and instant message their friends on the computer all at the same time. It's amazing. But it is questionable how well they can concentrate on any one of those things or even how much they can remember as a result when they are involved in doing so many different things at one time.

So I guess there are still some things, like studying, and doing homework, that are still better left to single-tasking. But when it comes to more simple things requiring less thought and concentration, like walking and chewing gum, I think most people should be able to do them both at the same time.

Good-Bye Summer

Last week, we officially said good-bye to summer and hello to fall. As difficult as it is for many of us to believe, September 21 marked the first day of the fall season. Another summer has come and gone and cooler weather, accompanied by the changing color of the leaves, is right around the corner. I have to admit that although I am happy to see the arrival of fall, I do feel a little sad about saying good-bye to summer.

Please don't get me wrong. I am really excited about the prospects of cooler weather. But I also realize that once summer is over, it's over, and it will be quite a while before it will be back. I will miss a lot of things about summer but especially the intense blue skies and sunshine of warm summer days, spending time outdoors, and the smell of flaming charcoal while cooking the evening dinner out on the grill.

Now, there are a few things about the summer season that I will not miss. For example, the past summer's heat at times was exceptionally brutal and that sweltering heat will not be missed at all. Nor will the air-conditioning bills that I received for the months of July and August. I won't miss stepping over the mounds of fire ant hills in the yard or having to mow the grass at least once every two weeks.

The soon-to-come first frost will hopefully relieve us of some of the annoying gnats, mosquitoes, flies, and fleas that I will not miss, either. The cooler weather will also send some of the other creepy crawly creatures beneath the ground looking for a safe place to spend their winter months.

Right now, the weather in beautiful southeastern North Carolina is in that typical transitioning period between summer and fall temperatures. At times during the day, it feels a little like fall and at times it still feels a little like summer. This transitioning weather seems to come with its own unique challenges. For example, this time of year, it is often difficult to know exactly how to dress.

The mornings are cool enough to warrant long sleeves but by midafternoon, it feels like short-sleeve weather again. Boxes containing sweaters, sweatshirts, and woolen garments are pulled out of storage but there is often a hesitancy to completely pack away the summer clothes. You can never be completely sure that there won't be a spell of warm weather ahead that is just not ready to let go.

During transitioning weather, air-conditioning controls and switches are probably tinkered with more than any other time of year. Frequently, the control switch is set to on then off, or the temperature is adjusted up and down throughout the day. The cool evenings tend to make for good open-window sleeping opportunities but by midday the next day, windows are closed tight with people opting for the relief of air-conditioning.

As for me, the refreshing temperatures of the past week have been enough to ignite total excitement about the onset of fall and "football weather"—cool, clear days and evenings so named because fall also brings us football season.

The animals sure seem to be enjoying the arrival of this cooler fall weather. My older dogs are acting many years younger, friskier than usual in the morning as they run and play in the yard. I have noticed the squirrels and birds scurrying about a lot more, hanging around the empty feeders in the yard. I guess that is their way of trying to get an important message to me. I also know that it won't be long before I will begin to see the annual flocks of birds as they make their way south, the cooler weather signaling them, as well, that it is that time of year again.

Yes, I will miss a lot about the summer, but I am really looking forward to fall for many reasons this year. I look forward to seeing the bright colorful leaves and sleeping under a warm blanket at night. I look forward to sitting on my front porch in a rocking chair on Friday evenings and listening to the distant roar of the crowd and the band playing during the local high school home games. At the end of October, Halloween evening will bring the much-welcomed sightings of little ghosts, pumpkins, and witches as they trick-or-treat their way down the street with their parents and flashlights.

Fall carnivals, warm apple cider, colorful mums and orange pumpkins are all ahead, too

So good-bye, summer and hello fall! I, for one, am glad you are finally here!

Lessons Learned in Albuquerque

My work has required extensive travel as of late. Most of my trips have been routine in nature, except for a recent experience at a hotel located in uptown Albuquerque, NM.

It was around 7:00 p.m., getting dark, and I had just returned from my walk to the Chili's Restaurant adjacent to my hotel. I entered my room, turned on the TV, and began to settle in to watch the evening news.

That was when I heard what sounded like a voice shouting something over a loud speaker. At first I thought it was just a part of the news show on the TV. Then I heard it again, even louder this time, and realized that it was actually coming from the direction of the hotel parking lot.

I pulled back the curtain and looked down from my sixth floor window. The parking lot was filled with people scurrying toward the hotel and surrounded by the flashing lights of police cars and fire trucks.

I opened the window slightly and listened.

"This is the Albuquerque police" was the message blaring over the loud speaker. "Everyone go into the hotel and stay inside your rooms."

The message continued to repeat until the parking lot of both the hotel and the restaurant were empty except for parked cars and emergency workers. Suddenly, a police helicopter appeared overhead and began to circle low over the hotel roof.

It was just like something from a movie.

We had been placed in a state of lockdown.

I decided to use the video recording device on my phone to capture what was happening. I uploaded the video to my Facebook page, wrote a short message describing what I was seeing outside my hotel, and sent it out on the internet.

What immediately followed was a series of comments coming from friends all over the country.

"Get away from that window young lady!" wrote a friend in Arkansas.

"Keep us posted, Lisa!" wrote another friend in Idaho.

"Are you okay?" was a message coming from Fayetteville.

"Saying a prayer, ma'am," wrote a friend from Hope Mills.

"Lisa, Lisa, what have you done now?" joked another friend.

These comments were followed by other messages from other friends in other states all across the country. Here I was in Albuquerque, yet my friends and family throughout the country knew exactly what was happening to me, in real time, and could actually see it on the video I posted. Strangely enough, I still had no clue why the hotel had been placed in a state of lockdown. I called the front desk but they said they did not know.

Then a message was posted from a friend in Greensboro, NC. She had checked the internet for breaking news in Albuquerque and discovered that there was a man with a gun running from police near the hotel. The police had surrounded him and had ordered the hotel and restaurant locked down because it was an immediate threat to public safety.

I watched out my window as two white vans pulled into the parking lot. Two members of what appeared to be a police SWAT team emerged from one of the vehicles. The officers were armed with backpacks and rifles, and they slowly began to make their way through the parking lot. They entered the front doors of the restaurant.

A few minutes later, I heard several explosions which later I learned came from police flash bombs. This was followed by shouts and several rifle shots. Then there was a period of silence except for the siren of one ambulance making its way down the street toward the hotel. Unfortunately, this situation did not have a happy ending. I found out the next morning that the gunman was killed by police in the alley just beside the hotel and restaurant.

With so many tragedies as of late, the event in Albuquerque made me take pause. We can never take our personal safety for granted. Tragedy can strike at any time and in any circumstance. Thanks to some brave men and women in law enforcement, it was fortunate that no others were hurt, especially with so many people in and around the busy hotel and restaurant.

This incident also reminded me of just how small and connected our world has become through technology and social media. I was able to share an experience one might only have imagined as "Breaking News" on television in real time with friends and family all over the country using a simple cell phone and a Facebook page.

Waiting

Last week, I was sitting in my car in a local fast food drive-through lane. I glanced at the clock on the dash. Just five minutes left until the transition from the breakfast menu to the lunch menu. I wanted breakfast. Evidently, so did everyone else. Cars were flying in the parking lot and whipping in line as if it were a NASCAR event.

I was in position number four. Car number one was at the speaker, the driver placing an order. I am not sure what he ordered but the wait seemed forever. Someone in a car behind me grew impatient and blew their horn. The driver at the speaker appeared oblivious. He was turning around to everyone in the car taking meal requests. Eventually, he placed his order and slowly pulled forward to the pick-up window.

I watched the same process continue as the two cars ahead of me each took their turn at the speaker. Finally, it was my turn. I eased up to the speaker and looked at the clock. The five-minute transition period had expired and it was now officially seven minutes into lunch. I crossed my fingers and asked, "Got any sausage biscuits left?"

"Sorry" was the reply. "We are serving lunch now. Can I take your order, please?"

Grumbling something about the long wait, I reluctantly placed my order. Of course, I understand my having to eat a cheeseburger for breakfast was my own fault. Obviously, I should have arrived a little earlier if I was determined to order from the breakfast menu. I am also well aware of the usual last minute breakfast rush, so I should have anticipated the wait. Even so, I was still disappointed.

Lately, I find it increasingly more difficult to wait to get what I want when I want it. Perhaps it is because we have become an "instant" society. We now have instant grits, instant oatmeal, instant coffee, instant tea, and instant messaging. Credit cards provide us with instant cash and fast food is just that, "fast food."

As technology advances, it increases our ability to get exactly what we want when we want it. We don't have to wait anymore. Computers provide us with access to instant information with the simple click of a mouse. In much the same fashion, television provides us with instant news and instant entertainment, cell phones and blackberries with instant anytime communication, and microwaves with instant food preparation. Convenience becomes expected and waiting patiently for something seems like some kind of primitive behavior of the past.

It doesn't seem all that long ago that we had to wait for things. I can remember my mother waiting hours for meat to thaw. If she forgot to take it out of the freezer in the morning, you could be sure we weren't having it for supper in the evening. We didn't have a microwave to nuke it in.

We didn't have a clothes dryer. We had to wait for sheets to dry outdoors on the clothesline. If it were raining, we had to wait to wash clothes on another day. We didn't have DVDs. We had to wait all year long for the one and only chance to watch the Wizard of Oz.

We surely didn't have e-mail, so we had to wait for the mail carrier each day. We didn't have the ability to print our pictures at home using memory cards or printer docks. We had to send our film off in the mail, wait for it to be developed and for the pictures to be returned. We didn't have pocket checks and ATMs. If we needed cash or needed to make a deposit, we would have to wait in line at the bank. And don't forget about the old "wait until your father gets home!" line.

Back then, however, waiting somehow didn't seem to be such a problem. Sometimes, the waiting and anticipating actually seemed to make things better when we did get things. When the meat thawed and mama finally fixed "slow food" without the aid of a microwave, it sure tasted good. It was worth the wait!

Fabric softeners have never successfully replaced that wonderful smell of climbing into a bed with clean sheets dried in the fresh air and sunshine. Possibly with the exception of Christmas morning and Halloween night, for which we also had to wait, watching the Wizard of Oz on television seemed like the most exciting two hours of the year.

It sure was fun to watch out for the mail carrier, when you were wishing and hoping for a special letter. Waiting in line at the bank, we got to know the tellers by name and spoke to friends that happened to be in line there, too. And the excitement of opening pictures arriving in the mail often equaled the thrill of seeing them for the first time.

It's hard to describe, but there is something rewarding in the feeling of anticipation and excitement that accompanies waiting for something worthwhile. My fear is that we are slowly losing that something in an increasingly instant society.

Thankfully, there are still some things for which we have to wait such as taking a drive to view colorful leaves in the fall, seeing our breath in the air from the chill of the first frost, watching the Super Bowl with friends and family, smelling daffodils blooming in the yard, and picking fresh strawberries in the spring. For me, all these are among the experiences that will be highly anticipated and well worth the wait. And sometime in the near future, I know my patience may once again be tried in a fast food drive-through lane. Maybe next time, I will just relax, turn on the radio, and simply enjoy the wait.

Classic Cars

I didn't know I was driving a classic car. I thought it was just a really, really old car. I figured my parents were making me drive it because they figured this was a way to teach me how to appreciate having a brand new car, when and if I ever earned enough money to buy one. Or, then again, I thought it could have been their form of a really cruel joke. Either way, I just chalked it up to having to drive the old clunker as a rite of passage into learning how to drive and becoming a responsible driver and car owner.

My classic car was a bright green '57 Chevrolet. For an old car, it was in mint condition. It had four doors and like the "Green Lantern," my classic car had a name. My friends affectionately referred to her as the "Green Bomb."

She had a sticker that someone had slipped on her rear bumper that read, "Don't honk! I'm peddling as fast as I can!" The steering wheel looked like a large green Hula-Hoop. And although I have never actually driven one, I equated driving her to what it must be like to drive a military tank. Of course, I upgraded the vehicle and equipped her with an eight-track tape player so we could listen to my favorite group, Three Dog Night, play "Joy to the World" as we cruised around town. Later, I went to college, the "Green Bomb" was sold and I finally got the brand new car I had wanted so much.

They say hindsight is 20/20.

Looking back, I am proud that I drove that classic old car in high school. I would give just about anything to have the old "Green Bomb" back in my driveway today, parked right beside my not-so-classic Toyota 4Runner.

Company Manners

In one way, fish and company are alike; they both start to stink after three days. I thought about that when I was recently invited to stay as a house guest for five days with some friends who live in Northwest Arkansas. I was there working for the week and they said that I would be much more comfortable in their home rather than spending an entire week in some stuffy old hotel room. I didn't want to impose but they very much insisted.

So, I decided to accept their gracious offer. Growing up, I was taught that there was a special set of manners one used when visiting as a guest. They were called company manners. Using your company manners, I was told, would increase the probability of being invited back for a future visit. So I worked hard that entire week to not wear out my welcome and use my best company manners.

The large two-story home where I stayed was situated in the peaceful, wooded countryside of Northwest Arkansas. The house was relatively new and absolutely beautiful both inside and out. To me, it looked like something right out of a Better Homes and Gardens magazine. Once inside, I was given the grand tour and taken up to the second floor. My hosts announced that I had the entire upstairs to myself for the week.

The upstairs consisted of three bedrooms and two bathrooms. I could choose whichever room I wanted. I looked around and discovered there was only one room that had a television, so that was the one I chose. My suitcase was brought up the spiral staircase and placed in my room. Then I was asked to make myself at home.

Unpacking my bag, I took a look around. On a table next to the bed, I noticed a pretty dish filled with candy, each piece individually wrapped in beautiful gold cellophane paper. Now company manners would not allow one to eat other people's food unless, of course, it was offered. This candy was so nicely displayed that I wasn't sure if it was put there for me or if it was part of the room decorations.

Temptation finally got the best of me. I tried one and it was delicious. I could have easily eaten the entire dish. However, I decided to limit myself to one a day. That way, there would be plenty left to spread around in the dish when I left so if they weren't there for me, it wouldn't look like I had eaten the decorations.

The bed in the room was made out of oak. It was obviously an antique and had an enormous headboard. The mattress was covered with a very expensive-looking orange floral bedspread. Including the two huge shams, there were exactly eleven decorative pillows on the bed, artistically arranged in a special pattern.

I tried my best to memorize how they looked before unmaking the bed. Company manners dictate that you must always put things back exactly the same way you found them. So I set my alarm clock ten minutes earlier than usual. I knew I would need at least that much extra time to get the bed looking the same in the morning.

I discovered there were two remote controls for the television and I fiddled around with them until I was finally able to turn the television on. When I travel, I have a habit of leaving the television on throughout the night in order to drown out strange and unusual noises. I found a movie that looked interesting, turned the volume down low, and eventually drifted off to sleep.

The next morning, I was up bright and early. First, I made the bed. I am not sure if I got it back exactly the same but it was pretty darn close. Next, I prepared to take a shower. In the bathroom, there were several fancy hand towels laid out across the vanity. Matching bath towels, in the same sequence of colors, hung neatly on hooks nearby. Now at my house, these would be considered the look-at towels.

Company manners would prevent you from using the look-at towels. So I searched around and found some regular, plain white towels in a linen closet. I turned on the water in the tub and looked for the shower button on the faucet to begin the shower. There wasn't one. I checked the showerhead to see if there was a switch. There wasn't one.

Now if I were in a hotel room, I would have called the front desk. But it was five thirty in the morning, I was a house guest and no one else was stirring. I decided the best, easiest, and most polite thing to do was to just to go ahead and take a bath.

After getting dressed, I was downstairs and ready to go ten minutes earlier than usual. Promptness is another important characteristic of good company manners. "Have trouble sleeping last night? I noticed the television was on really late into the evening" was the first thing I was asked. "I must have drifted off to sleep with the television on. Hope I didn't disturb you!" I replied.

My first mess up, I thought to myself. And for the rest of the week I slept each night with the television on but with the sound on mute. Each day, for five days, I was asked what I wanted to eat. Again I would try to use my company manners. That is one shouldn't be picky and be grateful for anything that is offered. So my standard response was that I liked everything.

My friends would proceed with a litany of choices. Again, I would respond that they all sounded good to me. This resulted in a really interesting week of cuisine ranging from Chinese orange shrimp in lettuce wraps and Chicken-Berry salad, to fresh fried Arkansas catfish. And being good company, I devoured it all.

I received an e-mail the other day from my friends in Arkansas. They thanked me for coming and actually told me that I was the perfect house guest. They said that they couldn't wait for me to come back and stay with them again. So I guess it is true. When you're visiting, it always pays to use your company manners.

My Gallimaufry Drawer

I was searching for a small screwdriver today in my gallimaufry drawer today.

Do you have a gallimaufry drawer in your home? If you aren't sure what one is, I'll give you a couple of hints. You probably have at least one of these drawers somewhere in your house right now. You may have several like we do. It is usually the very first place you go when you have misplaced something, and it is the very last place that you want your company to see.

According to Webster's dictionary, the word "gallimaufry" means hodgepodge. Whether we want to admit it or not, most everyone has a gallimaufry draw full of hodgepodge somewhere in their home. It is often referred to as the junk drawer. Sometimes it is just called "the drawer."

When something gets lost around our house, the first thing Mike asks is, "Did you look in the drawer?" Or if he is searching for something he can't find, he will tell me that he already checked the drawer and it wasn't in there. The gallimaufry drawer in our home is located in the kitchen next to the refrigerator. There is a ten-year accumulation of hodgepodge in this drawer. More stuff goes into the drawer than ever comes out of it and sometimes it jams when you try to open it. If I hold my mouth a certain way and jiggle the drawer up and down a little, I can usually get it to open. Worst case scenario, I squeeze my hand and wrist through the opening, feel around inside to find the item making it stick and dislodge it.

Today, after having to resort to the hand and wrist technique to get my gallimaufry drawer to open, I decided I would take the time to do an inventory of its contents. I have to admit the list was pretty impressive.

Located inside this one regular-sized kitchen drawer was one flashlight, two old VHS tapes, a small tin container full of small nails and screws, two rolls of undeveloped film, fifteen safety pins, a rusty dog chain, a balloon weight, two refrigerator magnets, three business cards, a pair of needle-nosed pliers, a night light, two screwdrivers, three mismatched earrings, a container of Chap Stick and $2.37 in change.

There was also an unopened set of foam earplugs, three dog collar batteries, a plastic aquarium plant, two air freshener plug-ins, four flashlight batteries, a dimmer switch, a comb, a ruler, two hair bands, one small candle, three countertop tile samples, two old campaign buttons, four pencils, sixteen pens, one set of chopsticks, one shotgun shell, an old thank you card, and a package of obviously forgotten "Forget-Me-Not" seeds.

Now I am not bragging, but I really wonder if there is anyone who could possibly have a better gallimaufry drawer than this one.

Please keep in mind that what I have described is our primary gallimaufry drawer. Most homes, including my own, also have a few secondary ones. A secondary gallimaufry drawer usually is a little more organized and tends to be more item-specific. Sometimes other things get thrown into them when we get in hurry to put things away, like when unexpected company arrives at the door.

For example, I have a secondary gallimaufry drawer located in a small chest in my entry hall. An item analysis of this particular drawer today revealed three picture albums, one picture frame, two pictures, one old newspaper article, a roll of blue painter's tape, and an electrical switch plate.

Obviously, this drawer was intended to be used for picture memorabilia, but the blue painter's tape, newspaper article, and electrical switch plate causes it to qualify for secondary gallimaufry drawer status.

I have seriously considered cleaning out the gallimaufry drawer in my kitchen. My fear is that if I did clean it out, I might not be able to locate what I need in the future.

And besides, where would I put all that stuff anyway?

Christmas Tree Shopping

I saw my first real Christmas tree of the season the other day. It was a large Fraser fir strapped across the top of a station wagon, slowly making its way through the intersection at Owen Drive and Boone Trail. More than likely, the tree was headed for someone's home to be decked out for the holidays.

We just brought home our new Christmas tree as well. However, it did not have to be tied to the roof of the car to be transported. The artificial Glacier Pine came in three sections, fit neatly inside a cardboard box and slid easily into the backseat of my Toyota. Our new artificial tree is pretty, but I really do miss having a real Christmas tree.

Growing up, we always had a real tree at Christmas time. We would purchase our tree from one of the local seasonal tree lots. We would always go as a family. Once we arrived at the lot, it would take a little time for us to pick out the perfect tree. Each row would be searched and every tree inspected before making the final decision. Trees were judged based on three criteria— straightness, fullness, and symmetry.

The Christmas tree lot always smelled of fresh cut pine. That smell is one of those wonderful aromas I have come to associate with the Christmas season. Since we did our tree shopping in the evening, there was usually a small fire burning in a metal barrel near the trailer where you paid for your tree. There you could stand and warm your hands while the chosen tree was secured to the top of the family car.

Once home, the Christmas tree was placed in a bucket of sugar water and leaned against the side of the house for a few days. Out of shear excitement, it was checked on and admired several times each day until finally being brought into the house for decorating.

As an adult, my eagerness to decorate in November has now caused me to resort to using an artificial Christmas tree. I learned a long time ago that it isn't smart to put up a real tree in November.

I tried putting one up on Thanksgiving Day about fifteen years ago. The tree dried out, turned brown, shed its needles, and became a fire hazard two weeks before Christmas. I had to take off all the decorations, take the tree down, and throw it away. I ended up buying another tree to replace it and then had to redecorate all over again. Ever since that disaster, I have used an artificial tree.

Our new tree is now out of the box, assembled, and fully decorated for the holidays. I was delighted to discover that with the lights and all the decorations, this tree does look amazingly real. It is straight, full, and symmetrical—all the characteristics we used to look for in the perfect tree at the Christmas tree lot.

All that seems to be missing is that special Christmas tree smell. That is why I sent Mike to a local seasonal tree lot to bring home a few discarded tree branches to use to decorate the fireplace mantel. Not only is the greenery festive, it also fills the living room with that familiar fragrance of fresh cut pine. It makes our artificial tree seem that much more real.

So with our beautiful tree up and decorated, it is really beginning to look a lot like Christmas around our house. And thanks to a few strategically placed tree boughs, it is also beginning to smell that way, too.

Dancing with the Stars

Lately, those reality television shows seem to be growing more and more popular. For whatever reason, I have never really been interested in watching them. I do have friends who watch a few of them and occasionally I will get a call asking me my opinion of something that happened on one of the shows. I usually laugh and explain how I don't watch reality TV.

No matter, a lengthy one-way conversation generally ensues with them explaining to me why this person or that person didn't deserve to get kicked off the island, how in their opinion Clay was better than Reuben, or why they believe the bachelor chose the wrong person. For the most part, I have listened politely, but to tell you the truth, I really couldn't care less.

Then one evening several weeks ago, all that changed. Someone called me and asked if I had ever watched the show Dancing with the Stars. Of course, I said no. They told me to go turn on the television.

"Why would I want to watch that?" I asked.

"Because Jerry Springer is dancing right now and you have got to see this!" was the reply. Now I have to admit at this point curiosity got the best of me.

I had watched a few Jerry Springer episodes in the past and I just could not imagine the king of rowdy talk shows doing the foxtrot. I turned on the television, found the station, and sure enough there was Jerry, all dressed up and dancing, if that is what you want to call it. I watched with great amusement as an obviously exhausted, out-of-breath Jerry and his partner finished up their dance and walked over to be judged.

To my amazement, the studio audience went absolutely wild and started chanting "Jerry, Jerry!" and from that moment on, I was hooked.

For those of you who have never watched Dancing with the Stars, it is basically a show that pairs a talented professional dancer with a star having no professional dancing experience. It is not always a movie or television star, it can be any famous star, like a professional ball player, a country-western singer, or even a well-known television news anchor. The object of the contest is to have the professional dancer work with the star over a period of weeks to see which one of the pairs eventually emerges to become judged as the best overall dance team. The dances the stars have to learn are pretty complex. They can range from the tango and the waltz to my personal favorite, the quickstep. During the competition each week, the team faces three tough judges that rate their performance on a one to ten scale and give them honest feedback on how they are progressing, and how they can improve. Later, the television viewing audience can also call in their votes on a toll free number and the viewers' votes can actually outweigh the decisions of the professional judges.

I guess that is why Jerry Springer stayed in the competition as long as he did this season. Amazingly, he didn't fall out of the total competition until very near the end and relatively speaking, the man couldn't dance. I believe that we, the television audience, just called in and voted for him because we liked his personality. Plus he was downright comical to watch. Eventually, however, even Jerry's charming personality could not save him from getting the boot.

For weeks, I continued to watch Dancing with the Stars as one by one contestants were eliminated from the competition. At the very end, the final two contestants were Mario Lopez and Emmitt Smith. The handsome Mario was a former kid star who played on the television series Saved by the Bell and the personable Emmitt Smith, was a former professional football star.

Both performed well throughout the entire season but I had grown to admire Emmitt's strong determination, continuous will to improve, and especially his winning attitude, even though deep down I thought Mario had more of an innate gift and seemed to be a natural dancer. On the final show, both stars did an unbelievably stellar performance and they both looked very much like trained professionals.

However, I actually stood and clapped with the studio audience when Emmitt and his partner were announced as the winners of the 2006 "Dancing with the Stars" competition! I was really happy to see him win because what Emmitt did during this competition was to affirm something that is extremely important for us all to remember. Being a winner isn't always easy. For the most part, it results from determination, hard work, tremendous effort, and a positive attitude. Emmitt Smith proved that, in the long run, it is really difficult to tell the difference between polished effort and innate ability.

Andy Griffith

The passing of TV legend Andy Griffith brought a sense of sadness for many longtime fans. For me, it felt like another chapter of life closed. It was a chapter scripting a past but not-so-long-ago time in my life when neighbors knew one another, front porch sitting was a favorite pastime, and recreation was as simple as a game of checkers or a Sunday afternoon car ride in the country.

It was a time when families sat down together each night at the supper table, TV was black and white, and a handshake was as good as your word. It was a time when people would drop by your home for no other reason than to say hello, and jaywalking was considered a crime.

Like most people, I didn't know Andy Griffith personally but I felt as though I did. After all, I spent many a night as a child glued in front of the television set in our home, watching a thirty-minute episode of The Andy Griffith Show.

I also felt as if I knew all the other colorful characters of Mayberry—Opie, Barney, Aunt Bea, Floyd the Barber, Gomer, Goober, Otis, and Thelma Lou—as well as those that appeared on special episodes from time to time, like the Darling family and my all-time favorite, the rock-slinging Ernest T. Bass. What kid did not run through the neighborhood at least once back in the day shouting "It's me! It's me! It's Ernest T.!"?

The uniqueness surrounding The Andy Griffith Show was that while we laughed and were entertained as we watched, we were also being reminded of many valuable life lessons, such as the immeasurable worth of human dignity, respect for differences, and the importance of caring about one another in both good times and in bad.

The show dealt with poignant lessons about truth, honesty, and character, and how a little common sense can go a long way in solving problems. With each episode of the show, we were reminded that there are indeed clear lines between what is right and what is wrong and that justice, when administered fairly, does not always mean equal.

We have lost Andy Griffith but fortunately for us, his iconic show can live on through reruns. Without doubt, both the late Andy Griffith and The Andy Griffith Show have served as great ambassadors for our fair state. Even with Barney's never-ending blunders or Otis's occasional "snootful," the show always depicted us North Carolinians as kind, gentle, neighborly souls with a love of God and country, guided by a strong sense of morals and values.

In my travels, I am often asked if there is really a town called Mayberry in North Carolina.

My standard response is that there is no Mayberry but there are many small towns in North Carolina that are much like Mayberry.

There is no Mount Pilot, I tell them.

But there is a Pilot Mountain.

However, there is a Siler City and we actually do take occasional trips "up to Raleigh."

Ironically, a gentleman approached me following a presentation I had given in another state not very long ago. He said he couldn't help but think about The Andy Griffith Show throughout my presentation. He added that he hoped that I didn't take offense to his comment.

"Was it my southern accent, or did I unconsciously slip with a colloquialism?" I asked.

"Neither," he said. "You took a complicated idea and made it simple. You know, like Andy Griffith did."

No, his comment did not offend me at all.

In fact, I considered it to be quite an honor.

CPSIA information can be obtained at www.ICGtesting.com
Printed in the USA
LVOW08s2226060215

426021LV00032B/2428/P